BANNERS, BUTTONS AND SONGS

A Pictorial Review and Capsule Almanac of

America's Presidential Campaigns

AF700034

Compiled and Annotated by

HENRY PAPALE

PHOTOS
CAMPAIGN SONGS
STATISTICS
CARTOONS
SLOGANS
SPEECH EXCERPTS
WITH EQUAL TIME FOR WINNERS AND LOSERS SINCE 1789

ST. MARTIN'S PRESS / NEW YORK

BANNERS, BUTTONS AND SONGS. Copyright © 1968, 1984 by Henry Papale. All rights reserved. Printed in the United States of America. No part of this book may be used or reproduced in any manner whatsoever without written permission except in the case of brief quotations embodied in critical articles or reviews. For information, address St. Martin's Press, 175 Fifth Avenue, New York, N.Y. 10010.

ISBN 0-312-06633-3

Library of Congress Catalog Number: 84-50784

A production of St. Ives Publications, Ltd.

Layout by **Marcia Dente**
Edited by **Roberta Williams Papale**

In the beginning...

. . . there were no conventions or whistle-stop tours; there were no buttons, no campaign songs. In the beginning the popular vote meant little, and in both of George Washington's elections there was only one candidate and one party. The Presidential Campaign developed along with the country. As America changed from a relatively small and simple agricultural-rural nation to a complex urbanized industrial giant of 200 million people the methods of choosing a candidate changed from the caucus of a few men to the conventions of thousands. The methods of campaigning changed from reserved statements published in newspapers (Monroe vs. King, 1816) to the exhausting whistle-stop campaigns initiated by William Jennings Bryan. Bryan spoke to more voters in any one of his campaigns than did all the candidates in the first eight elections, but even his efforts seem dwarfed when seen in the light of the Nixon-Kennedy television debates of the 1960 campaign. It has been estimated that at least 100 million persons viewed each of these debates! Suffice it to say: campaign methods are still changing, still developing.

So many different and seemingly unrelated elements combine to make the Presidential Campaign the colorful spectacle that it is that the problem facing the compiler of any book dealing with this subject is more a question of what to include rather than what to exclude. Portions of the Inaugural Addresses of each President are included because each Address seems to be studded with one or more concepts that are either timeless in their application to Democracy (as President Polk's Address) or startling when viewed in historical perspective (as President Taft's Address). Pictures (photographs and prints) and other memorabilia of both winners and losers have been included. This has been done not so much for the winners as for the losers who are usually relegated to a rather unfair state of oblivion.

Sometimes a campaign is remembered for one outstanding event as is the Tilden-Hayes bout of 1876 with its disputed votes, while other campaigns like the "Free Soil" of 1848 leave only a slogan. Whatever the case may be, the outstanding features have been noted and/or illustrated whenever possible. The book also includes reproductions of elements that are on the periphery of the campaign, e.g., a reproduction of the Invitation to President Jackson's Inaugural Ball, or the Thomas Nast cartoons that introduced the Donkey and the Elephant as party symbols.

Directly concerning the conventions, the reader will find that on occasion the number of ballots cast to nominate a candidate is noted. This is done to illustrate that conventions were not always the simple one or two ballot affairs of recent years.

Finally there is that peculiar animal, the Campaign Song. Ever since Martin Van Buren and the Democrats were "sung down" by Harrison and his Whigs in the "Hard Cider Campaign" of 1840 no man has won or lost a presidential election without from one to a hundred campaign songs in his campaign baggage along with his standard paraphernalia of buttons, banners, slogans, and badges, and hats, and canes, and stickers, etc., etc. The songs are usually very long; therefore only short excerpts are printed here. There were songs written for and against every candidate and sometimes (notably Van Buren, "Harrison the Second," and Bryan) the songs against the candidates are more interesting (textually) and seem to be more illustrative of the general mood of the campaign than those written for him. Some non-campaign songs of the patriotic genre have been included (under Adams, Madison, Monroe, and Jackson) because they take on a new interest historically when they are identified with a President's tenure. Further, these songs were and are sung at political gatherings and, unlike the thousands of specifically political songs, they have endured throughout our history.

There are certain policies of format used throughout the book that may need some explanation; when the birth, death, and state is given for each candidate, for example:

James G. Blaine (1830-1893) of Pennsylvania

the state is always the state of birth, and not the state which the candidate may have spent most of his life representing in public office.

Banners, Buttons, and Songs is a pictorial history and capsule almanac of Presidential Campaigns since 1789. It is an attempt to capture in a many-faceted visual way the peripheral as well as the central elements that make a "four year madness" out of the serious business of choosing a nominee and electing a President, an attempt to produce an interesting factual supplement to Presidential Campaign History.

Henry Papale

1789 & 1792

President:
GEORGE WASHINGTON[1]
(1732-1799) of Virginia

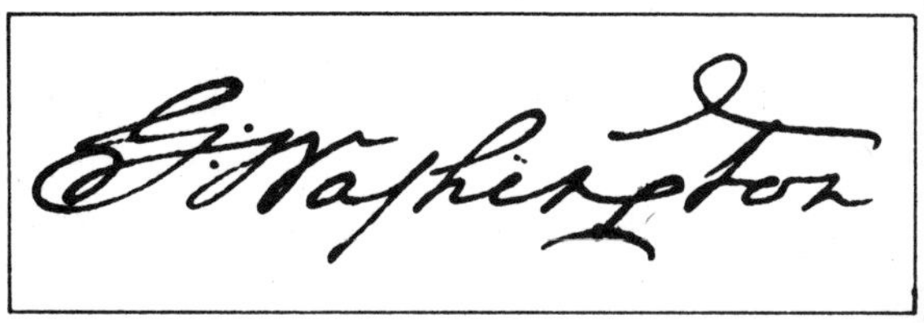

PREVIOUS OCCUPATIONS

Surveyor
Army (French & Indian War)
House of Burgesses
Continental Congress
General of the Army (Revolutionary War)

Vice-President: John Adams
Party: Federalist
Popular Vote: unknown
Electoral Vote: (1789) 69
(1792) 132

EXCERPT FROM 1st INAUGURAL ADDRESS, APRIL 30, 1789:

". . . I behold the surest pledges, that as, on one side, no local prejudices or attachments, no separate views, nor party animosities, will misdirect the comprehensive and equal eye which ought to watch over this great assemblage of communities and interests; so on another, that the foundations of our national policy will be laid in the pure and immutable principles of private morality; and the pre-eminence of free government be exemplified by all the attributes which can win the affections of its citizens, and command the respect of the world . . ."

[1] The elections of 1789 and 1792 were unlike any that followed in that Washington had no opponents, there were no campaigns, and no party of opposition had been established. There were even movements to crown Washington and to address him as Excellency; it is to Washington's credit that he repressed such monarchistic movements so that they could never again be raised. It is interesting to note that during Washington's tenure in office, New York (1st term) and then Philadelphia (2nd term) served as the capital cities. Not until the end of John Adams' term was the District of Columbia established as the permanent seat of the Federal Government.

1796

President:
JOHN ADAMS
(1735-1826) of Massachusetts

PREVIOUS OCCUPATIONS

State Legislature
Continental Congress
Ambassador (to France, Netherlands, Britain)
Vice President

EXCERPT FROM INAUGURAL ADDRESS, MARCH 1, 1797:

". . . There may be little solidity in an ancient idea that congregations of men into cities and nations are the most pleasing objects in the sight of superior intelligences, but this is very certain, that to a benevolent human mind there can be no spectacle presented by any nation more pleasing, more noble, more majestic, or august, than an assembly like that which has so often been seen in this and the other Chamber of Congress, of a Government in which the executive authority as well as that of all the branches of the Legislature, are exercised by citizens selected at regular periods by their neighbors to make and execute laws for the general good . . ."

Vice-President: Thomas Jefferson
Party: Federalist[1]
Popular Vote: unknown[2]
Electoral Vote: Adams 71
Jefferson 68

HAIL, COLUMBIA

Although there were no real Campaign Songs until 1840, many of our favorite patriotic songs were written during the early years of our Nation. "Hail, Columbia" was written by Joseph Hopkinson in the midst of an upsurge of patriotic fervor which occurred during a series of naval crises with France in 1798.

[1]*The election of 1796 was the first in which there were two political parties, the Federalist led by Adams, and the Democratic-Republican led by Jefferson.*

[2]*In only six of the sixteen states did the people cast votes for electors; the other ten had their electors chosen by their state legislatures. All the presidential candidates from Washington to John Quincy Adams were chosen by congressional caucus; it wasn't until Andrew Jackson was nominated by the Tennessee State Legislature that the caucus method ended.*

[3]*There were actually thirteen candidates who received electoral votes in this election including Thomas Pinckney of South Carolina (59) and Samuel Adams (President Adams' cousin) of Massachusetts (15); even George Washington received 2 votes.*

1800 & 1804

President:
THOMAS JEFFERSON[1]
(1743-1826) of Virginia

PREVIOUS OCCUPATIONS

Lawyer
House of Burgesses
Continental Congress
Governor
Ambassador (to France)
Secretary of State
Vice President

Vice-President:
Aaron Burr (1st term)
George Clinton (2nd term)

Party:
Democratic-Republican

Popular Vote: unknown
Electoral Vote: (1800) 73[2]
(1804) 162[3]

EXCERPT FROM 1st INAUGURAL ADDRESS, MARCH 4, 1801:

". . . Equal and exact justice to all men, of whatever state or persuasion, religious or political; peace, commerce, and honest friendship with all nations . . ."

---

[1] *Jefferson and John Adams were the only two presidents who were also signers of the Declaration of Independence.*

[2] *The complete electoral tally was: Jefferson 73, Burr 73, Adams 65, C. C. Pinckney 64, Jay 1. There being a tie between Jefferson and Burr, the election was thrown to the House of Representatives. It took 36 ballots and seven days to elect Jefferson. Burr was named Vice-President.*

[3] *Jefferson's opponent was Charles Cotesworth Pinckney, Federalist from South Carolina; Pinckney received 14 electoral votes. In this election Clinton was specifically nominated for the office of Vice-President so that no longer would vice-presidents be the second best vote-getter in the presidential race.*

1808 & 1812

President:
JAMES MADISON
(1751-1836) of Virginia

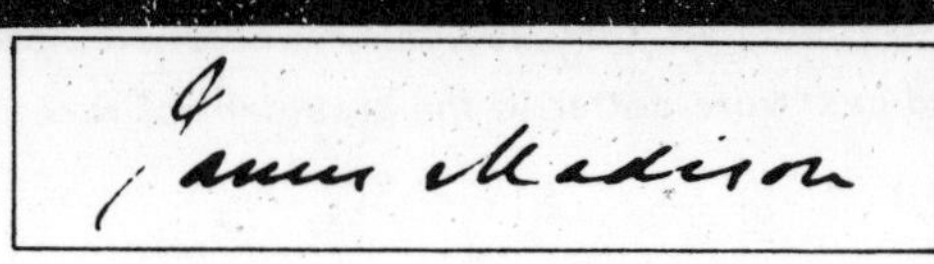

PREVIOUS OCCUPATIONS
State Legislature
Continental Congress
Congressman
Secretary of State

LOSING CANDIDATES:
(1808): C. C. Pinckney
(1812): De Witt Clinton
Party: Federalist
Popular Vote: unknown
Electoral Vote: (1808) 47, (1812) 89

Vice-President:
George Clinton (1st term)
Elbridge Gerry (2nd term)
Party: Democratic-Republican
Popular Vote: unknown
Electoral Vote: (1808) 122
(1812) 128

EXCERPT FROM 1st INAUGURAL ADDRESS, MARCH 4, 1809:

". . . to avoid the slightest interference with the right of conscience or the functions of religion, so wisely exempted from civil jurisdiction; to preserve in their full energy the other salutary provisions in behalf of private and personal rights, and of the freedom of the press; . . . to keep within the requisite limits a standing military force, always remembering that an armed and trained militia is the firmest bulwark of republics . . ."

THE STAR-SPANGLED BANNER

Our National Anthem was written by Francis Scott Key in 1812 during the bombardment of Fort McHenry.

O say, can you see, by the dawn's early light,
What so proudly we hailed at the twilight's last gleaming?
Whose broad stripes and bright stars, through the perilous fight,
O'er the ramparts we watched, were so gallantly streaming!
And the rockets' red glare, the bombs bursting in air,
Gave proof through the night that our flag was still there:
O say, does that star-spangled banner yet wave
O'er the land of the free and the home of the brave?

1816 & 1820

President:
JAMES MONROE[1]
(1758-1831) of Virginia

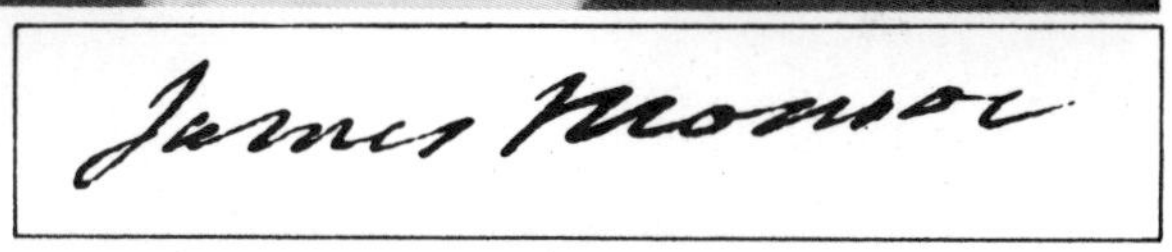

PREVIOUS OCCUPATIONS

Army (Revolutionary War)
State Legislature
Continental Congress
Senator
Governor
Ambassador (to Britain)
Secretary of State

LOSING CANDIDATES:
1816: Rufus King (Federalist)
1820: John Quincy Adams (D.-R.)
(Monroe was virtually unopposed in 1820 and Adams received only one electoral vote.)

Vice-President:
Daniel D. Tompkins
Party: Democratic-Republican
Popular Vote: unknown
Electoral Vote: (1816) 183
(1820) 231

EXCERPT FROM THE MONROE DOCTRINE:

". . . We owe it therefore to candor, and to the amicable relations existing between the United States and those powers that we should consider any attempt on their part to extend their system to any portion of this Hemisphere as dangerous to our peace and safety . . ."

HAIL TO THE CHIEF

The official "President's March" was written in 1812 and began to become identified with the Chief Executive during the administration of Monroe. It was originally a setting of a poem by Sir Walter Scott; the composer was James Sanderson; it is only Sanderson's music that is heard today.

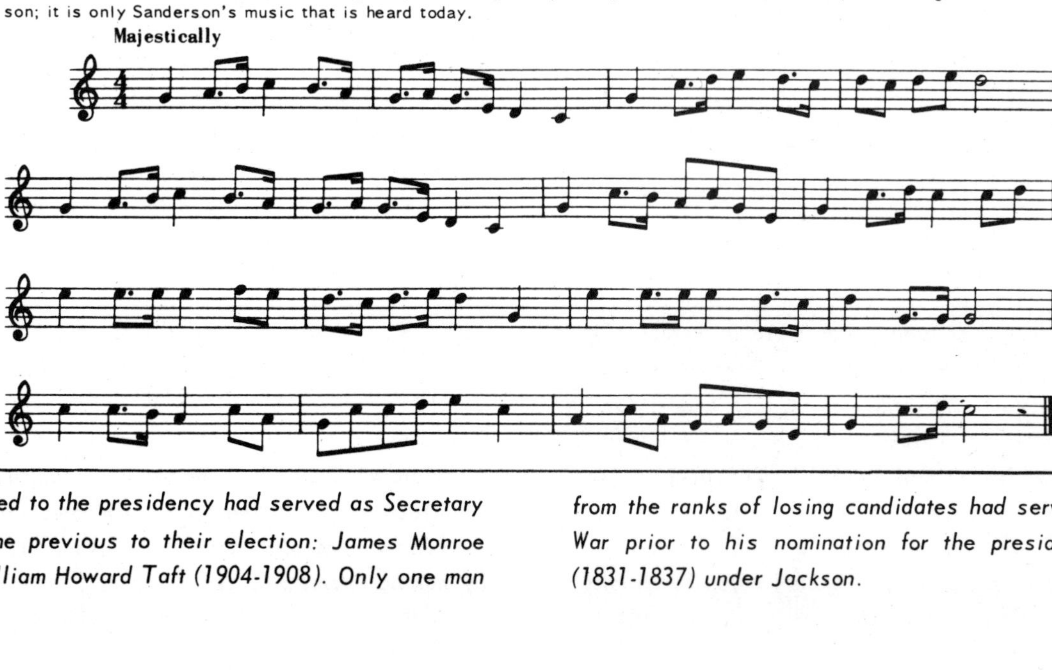

[1]*Only two men elected to the presidency had served as Secretary of War at some time previous to their election: James Monroe (1814-1815) and William Howard Taft (1904-1908). Only one man from the ranks of losing candidates had served as Secretary of War prior to his nomination for the presidency: Lewis Cass (1831-1837) under Jackson.*

1824

President:
JOHN QUINCY ADAMS
(1767-1848) of Massachusetts

PREVIOUS OCCUPATIONS

Ambassador (to Netherlands, Portugal, Prussia, Russia, Britain)
State Legislature
Senator
Secretary of State
Congressman (after his Presidency for 17 years)

LOSING CANDIDATES:
Andrew Jackson (Democrat); Electoral Vote: 99
Henry Clay (Democrat); Electoral Vote: 37
(In the popular vote, Jackson received 155,872; Clay 47,217; and another candidate, Crawford 46,979.)

Vice-President:
John C. Calhoun
Party:
National Republican
Popular Vote: 105,321[1]
Electoral Vote: 84[2]

EXCERPT FROM INAUGURAL ADDRESS, MARCH 4, 1825:

". . . It is a source of gratification and of encouragement to me to observe that the great result of this experiment upon the theory of human rights has at the close of that generation by which it was formed been crowned with success equal to the most sanguine expectations of its founders. Union, justice, tranquility, the common defense, the general welfare, and the blessings of liberty—all have been promoted by the Government under which we have lived. Standing at this point of time, looking back to that generation which has gone by and forward to that which is advancing, we may at once indulge in grateful exultation and in cheering hope . . ."

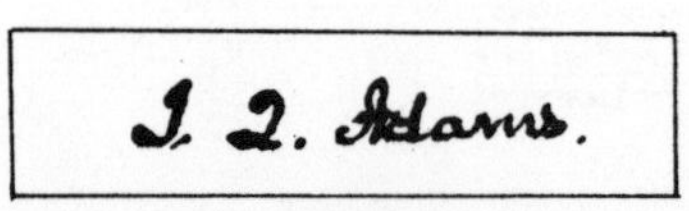

[1] *This "popular vote count" is highly inaccurate in representing the popular sentiment because: 1) Only five states represented all four candidates at the polls. 2) Six states had three tickets. 3) Seven states had only two tickets. 4) Six states (including populous New York which backed Adams) had electors chosen by the legislature. 5) North Carolina had a "fusion ticket" for Jackson and Adams and the count (wrongly) gives all these votes to Jackson. 6) The percentage of eligible voters who actually voted was sometimes under 10%, e.g., Pennsylvania's more than 1,000,000 inhabitants cast a mere 47,000 votes while Virginia's 625,000 cast only 15,000 votes.*

[2] *The original electoral vote stood thus: Adams 84, Jackson 99, Crawford 41, Clay 37. There being no majority for any candidate, the election went to the House of Representatives and produced the following result: Adams 87, Jackson 71, Crawford 54, thereby making Adams president.*

President: ANDREW JACKSON

1828

(1767-1845) of South Carolina

Vice-President: John C. Calhoun
Party: Democrat[1]
Popular Vote: 647,231
Electoral Vote: 178

EXCERPT FROM 1st INAUGURAL ADDRESS, MARCH 4, 1829:

". . . Considering standing armies as dangerous to free governments in time of peace, I shall not seek to enlarge our present establishment, nor disregard that salutary lesson of political experience which teaches that the military should be held subordinate to the civil power . . . . As long as our Government is administered for the good of the people, and is regulated by their will; as long as it secures to us the rights of person and of property, liberty of conscience and of the press, it will be worth defending; and so long as it is worth defending,a patriotic militia will cover it with an impenetrable aegis . . ."

LOSING CANDIDATE:
John Quincy Adams
Party: National Republican
Popular Vote: 509,097
Electoral Vote: 83

MY COUNTRY, 'TIS OF THEE

(Written in 1831)

Samuel Francis Smith, 1808-95

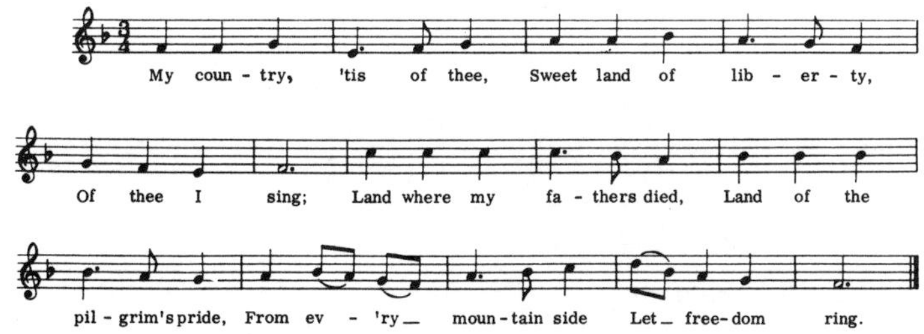

[1] *The name "Democrat" was used for the first time in this campaign.*

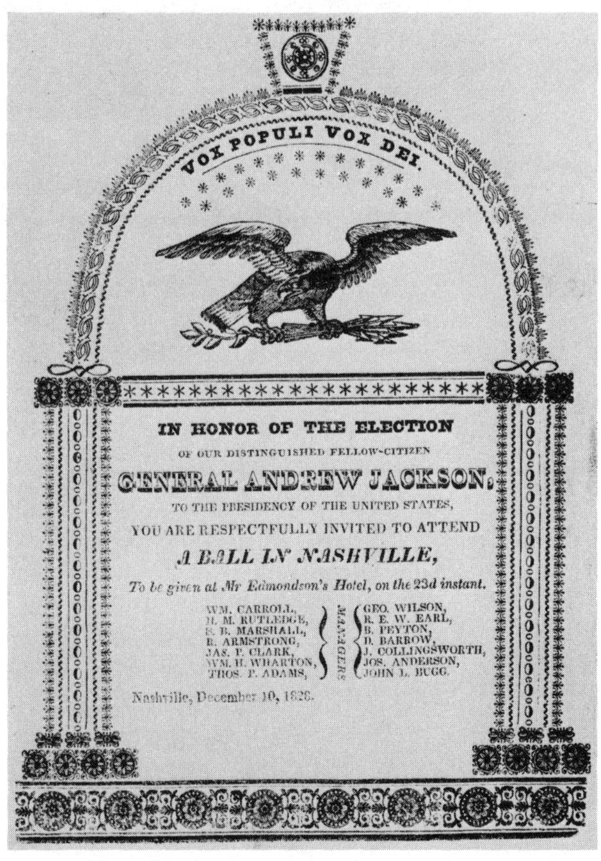

VOX POPULI VOX DEI.

IN HONOR OF THE ELECTION
OF OUR DISTINGUISHED FELLOW-CITIZEN
GENERAL ANDREW JACKSON,
TO THE PRESIDENCY OF THE UNITED STATES,
YOU ARE RESPECTFULLY INVITED TO ATTEND
A BALL IN NASHVILLE,
To be given at Mr Edmondson's Hotel, on the 23d instant.

WM. CARROLL,
H. M. RUTLEDGE,
R. B. MARSHALL,
R. ARMSTRONG,
JAS. P. CLARK,
WM. H. WHARTON,
THOS. P. ADAMS,
MANAGERS
GEO. WILSON,
R. E. W. EARL,
B. PEYTON,
D. BARROW,
J. COLLINGSWORTH,
JOS. ANDERSON,
JOHN L. BUGG.

Nashville, December 10, 1828.

Invitation to Jackson's Inaugural Ball.

1832

Losing Candidate:
HENRY CLAY
(1777-1852) of Virginia

OCCUPATION OF CANDIDATE:
Politician

POLITICAL OFFICES HELD:
Kentucky State Legislature
U. S. Senator, Ky.
U. S. House of Representatives
Secretary of State

Running Mate:
John Sergeant
Party:
National Republican
Convention: Baltimore
Popular Vote: 530,189
Electoral Vote: 49

Clay shares with William Jennings Bryan the rather dubious distinction of having lost three campaigns (1824, 1832, and 1844). He stands alone in that he is the only three time loser to have lost each campaign while representing a different party every time (Democratic-Republican, National Republican, and Whig).

1832

President: *ANDREW JACKSON*

"OLD HICKORY"

Vice-President: Martin Van Buren
Party: Democrat
Convention: Baltimore[1]
Popular Vote: 687,502
Electoral Vote: 219

PREVIOUS OCCUPATIONS

Army (Revolutionary War)
Lawyer
Congressman (Tennessee)
Senator
State Supreme Court Justice
Army (War of 1812: General)

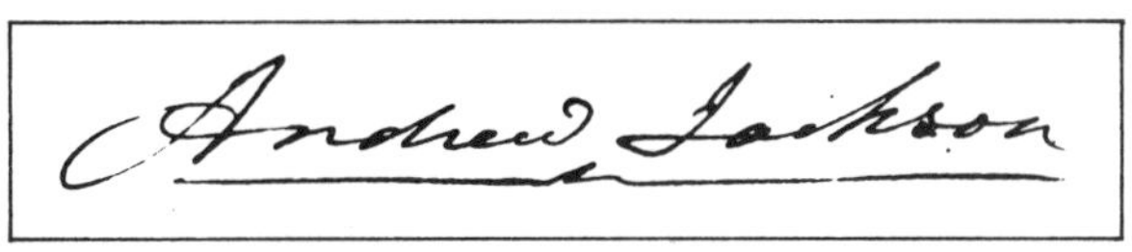

EXCERPT FROM 2nd INAUGURAL ADDRESS, MARCH 4, 1833:

"... Great is the stake placed in our hands; great is the responsibility which must rest upon the people of the United States. Let us realize the importance of the attitude in which we stand before the world. Let us exercise forebearance and firmness. Let us extricate our country from the dangers which surround it, and learn wisdom from the lessons they inculcate ..."

"KING ANDREW THE FIRST"

The political cartoonist has not only been a mirror of public sentiment (e.g., Keppler's lampooning of Benjamin Harrison, or the "King Andrew" reproduced here), but has sometimes helped to shape public opinion thus forcing positive action, as did Thomas Nast with his Boss Tweed cartoons in the latter half of the nineteenth century. The circumstances that prompted "King Andrew the First" can be briefly summed up as follows. Jackson seemed to be exceeding the bounds of executive power outlined in the Constitution to such an extent that cries of "dictator" and "monarch" began to be heard. One example of Jackson's power during his second term was his private and relentless war on the Second Bank of the United States. He managed to close the bank and further antagonized his enemies by distributing the defunct institution's funds like piratical booty to various state banks.

[1] *The 1832 election was the first preceded by National Party Conventions.*

1836

Losing Candidate: *WILLIAM HENRY HARRISON*

(1773-1841) of Virginia

PREVIOUS OCCUPATIONS

Army
Secretary of Northwest Territory
Governor (Territory of Indiana)
Army (War of 1812: Major General)

Running Mate: Francis Granger
Party: Whig[1]
Convention: Harrisburg[2]
Popular Vote: 549,567
Electoral Vote: 73

Reproduced below are a few of the covers of the hundreds of songs written for Harrison for his successful campaign of 1840.

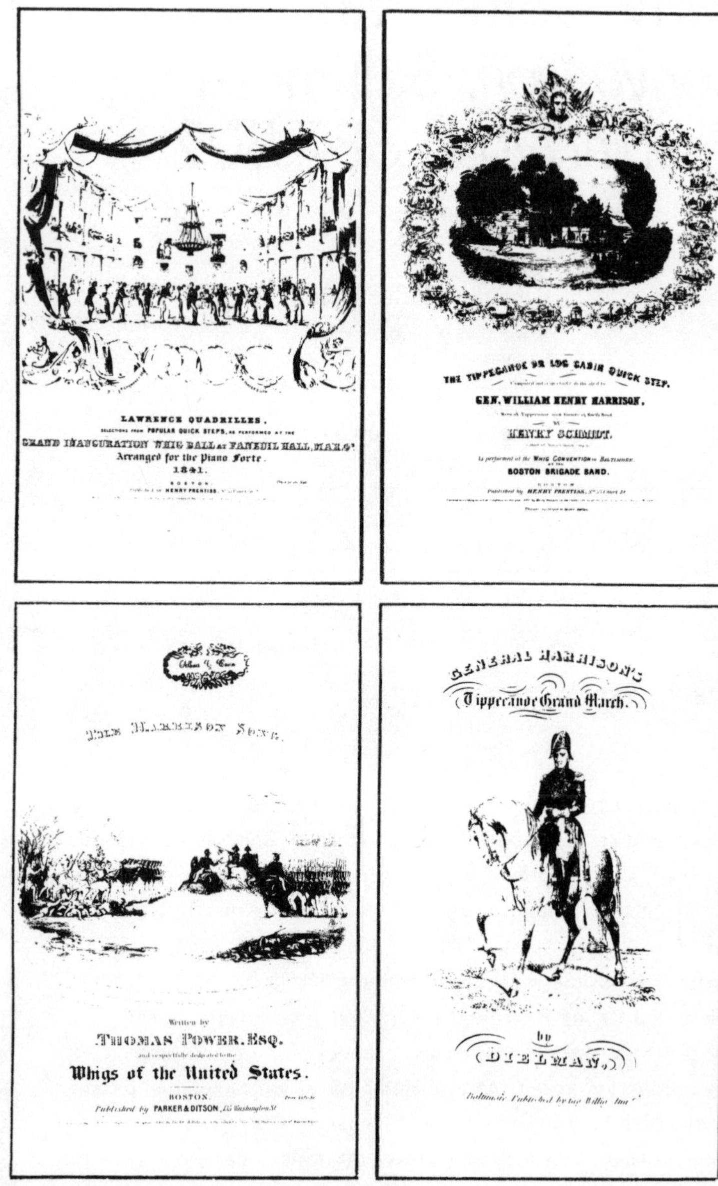

---

[1]The name "Whig" was seen in print for the first time in Niles's Register of April, 1834, to designate the party in opposition to the Democrats in the states of Connecticut and New York.

[2]This convention was called by a "third" party, the Anti-Masons, who merged with the newly-formed Whigs and other anti-Jackson groups, all of whom backed Harrison, excepting a portion of voters from New England who voted for Daniel Webster (he received 41,287 popular votes).

1836

President: MARTIN VAN BUREN

(1782-1862) of New York

Vice-President: Richard M. Johnson[1]
Party: Democrat
Convention: Baltimore
Popular Vote: 761,549
Electoral Vote: 170

PREVIOUS OCCUPATIONS

Lawyer
State Legislature
Senator
Governor
Secretary of State
Vice President

GRAND MATCH BETWEEN THE KINDERHOOK PONEY AND THE OHIO PLOUGHMAN

Published April 1836 by the proprietor H. R. Robinson 18 Cortland St. New York

EXCERPT FROM INAUGURAL ADDRESS, MARCH 4, 1837:

". . . Occasionally, it is true, the ardor of public sentiment, outrunning the regular progress of the judicial tribunals or seeking to reach cases not denounced as criminal by the existing law, has displayed itself in a manner calculated to give pain to the friends of free government and to encourage the hopes of those who wish for its overthrow. These occurrences, however, have been far less frequent in our country than in any other of equal population on the globe, and with the diffusion of intelligence it may well be hoped that they will constantly diminish in frequency and violence. The generous patriotism and sound common sense of the great mass of our fellow-citizens will assuredly in time produce this result; for as every assumption of illegal power not only wounds the majesty of the law, but furnishes a pretext for abridging the liberties of the people, the latter have the most direct and permanent interest in preserving the landmarks of social order and maintaining on all occasions the inviolability of those constitutional and legal provisions which they themselves have made . . ."

---

[1] *Because no vice-presidential candidate had a majority of electoral votes, Richard M. Johnson became the only man to be chosen Vice-President by the Senate.*

1840

Losing Candidate:
MARTIN VAN BUREN

"THE LITTLE MAGICIAN OF THE KINDERHOOK"

Running Mate: **Richard M. Johnson**
Party: **Democrat**
Convention: **Baltimore**
Popular Vote: **1,128,702**
Electoral Vote: **60**

*While Harrison had more songs written **for** him than any other candidate, Van Buren probably had more songs written **against** him than any! "Who Is Martin Van Buren" is one of them. The tune is the same as that used for "Tyler and Tippecanoe." After the election Van Buren (or perhaps some other glum Democrat) is supposed to have said: "We were sung down, drunk down, and lied down," a statement with which all historians have heartily agreed.*

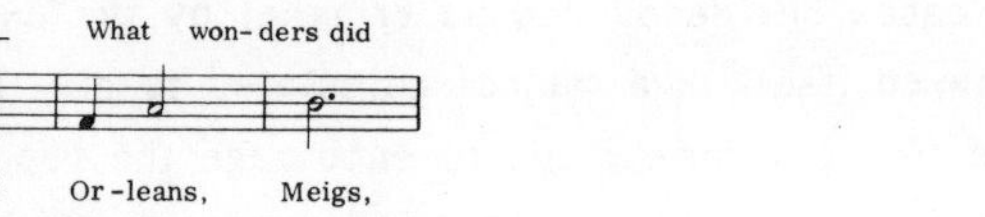

WHO IS MARTIN VAN BUREN

(Tune: Rosin the Beau)

President: WILLIAM HENRY HARRISON[1]

1840

Vice-President: John Tyler
Party: Whig
Convention: Baltimore
Popular Vote: 1,275,017
Electoral Vote: 234

EXCERPT FROM INAUGURAL ADDRESS, MARCH 4, 1841:

". . . Of all the great interests which appertain to our country, that of union—cordial, confiding, fraternal union—is by far the most important, since it is the only true and sure guaranty of all others . . ."

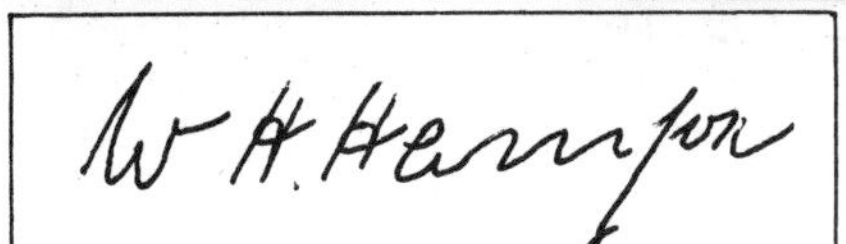

"TIPPECANOE AND TYLER TOO"

PREVIOUS OCCUPATIONS

Congressman
Senator
Governor
Vice President

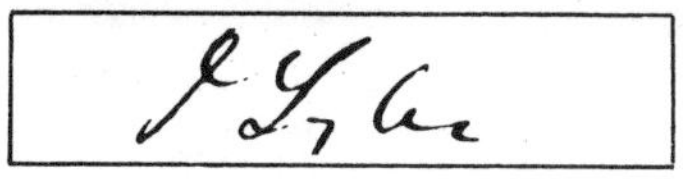

TYLER AND TIPPECANOE[2]

(Tune: Rosin the Beau)

[1]Harrison contracted pneumonia on his Inaugural Day and died after one month in office; Tyler succeeded him as President. There is little to say about Harrison except that his inaugural address was the longest delivered by any president; it is longer than all four of Franklin Delano Roosevelt's addresses put together.

[2]More campaign songs were written for Harrison than for any other president. All of the songs said the same thing. Some of the key words were: "log cabin," "cider," "frontier," and "hero." In this election the Campaign Song reached its height as an effective tool for winning votes, and the "Hard Cider Campaign" went down in history as the wildest singing, mudslinging, drinking, and slogan-making campaign of them all.

1844

Losing Candidate: HENRY CLAY

"I'D RATHER BE RIGHT THAN BE PRESIDENT"[1]

This excerpt is taken from Clay's last great speech before the Senate to urge compromise at all costs to preserve the Union. The date was July 22, 1850, and we are told, from eye-witnesses that great orator spoke to an enthralled audience for three hours!

". . . what is an individual man? An atom, almost invisible without a magnifying glass — a mere speck upon the surface of the immense universe — not a second in time, compared to immeasurable, never-beginning, and never-ending eternity; a drop of water in the great deep, which evaporates and is borne off by the winds; a grain of sand, which is soon gathered to the dust from which it sprung. Shall a being so small, so petty, so fleeting, so evanescent, oppose itself to the onward march of a great nation, to subsist for ages and ages to come — oppose itself to that long line of posterity which, issuing from our loins, will endure during the existence of the world? Forbid it, God! Let us look at our country and our cause; elevate ourselves to the dignity of pure and disinterested patriots, wise and enlightened statesmen, and save our country from all impending dangers. What if, in the march of this nation to greatness and power, we should be buried beneath the wheels that propel it onward? What are we — what is any man worth who is not ready and willing to sacrifice himself for the benefit of his country when it is necessary?"

Running Mate: Theodore Frelinghuysen
Party: Whig
Convention: Baltimore
Popular Vote: 1,299,068
Electoral Vote: 105

THE RISE AND ORIGIN OF THE AMERICAN CLAY

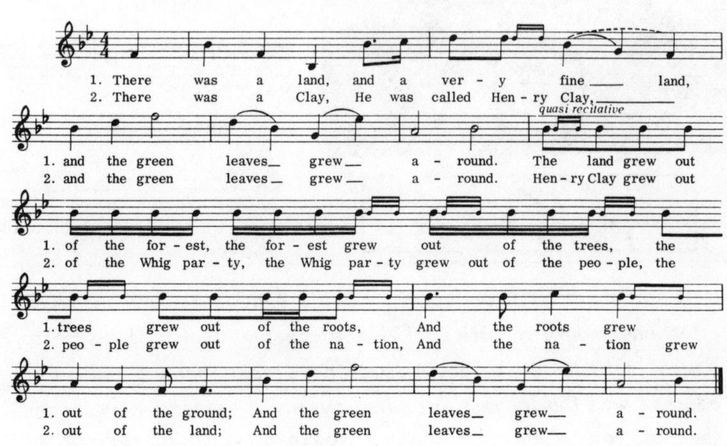

[1]*Although this was not Clay's slogan, it might well have been; the words were his own and proved to be prophetic.*

1844

President:
JAMES K. POLK
(1795-1849) of North Carolina

"FIFTY-FOUR FORTY OR FIGHT"[1]

Vice-President: George M. Dallas
Party: Democrat
Convention: Baltimore[2]
Popular Vote: 1,337,243
Electoral Vote: 170

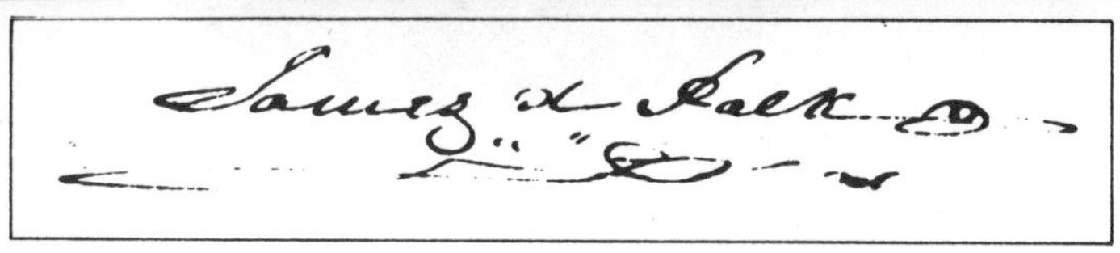

PREVIOUS OCCUPATIONS

State Legislature (Tennessee)
Congressman
Governor

EXCERPT FROM INAUGURAL ADDRESS, MARCH 4, 1845:

". . . By the theory of our Government majorities rule, but this right is not an arbitrary or unlimited one. It is a right to be exercised in subordination to the Constitution and in conformity to it. One great object of the Constitution was to restrain majorities from oppressing minorities or encroaching upon their just rights. Minorities have a right to appeal to the Constitution as a shield against such oppression . . ."

---

[1] *This slogan refers to the expansionist claims that all the Oregon territory to the Alaskan border, or 54°40', rightfully belonged to the U. S. The slogan was uttered after the election during the settlement of the issue to the 49th degree latitude. This was considerably less than the slogan called for.*

[2] *Polk was the first "dark horse" candidate. He polled nothing on the first seven ballots; on the eighth ballot he had 44. On the ninth ballot the first "stampede" in history occurred; when the balloting was over Polk had every vote.*

1848

Losing Candidate: *LEWIS CASS* [1]

(1782-1866) of New Hampshire

Running Mate: William O. Butler
Party: Democrat
Convention: Baltimore
Popular Vote: 1,299,068
Electoral Vote: 127

OCCUPATIONS OF CANDIDATE

Schoolteacher
Lawyer
State Legislature
Army (War of 1812)
Secretary of War
Senator

CASS AND BUTLER
(Tune: "Picayune Butler")

They come to town the other day
And told us what the People say --
Ahoo!
That Cass and Butler 'tis a fact,
O, they're the ones to clear the track,
Ahoo!
Cass and Butler's coming, coming,
Cass and Butler's come in town --
Cass and Butler's coming, coming,
Cass and Butler's come to town.
Ah, ou, ah ou, ah ou--ah ou, ah ou, ah ou!
Cass and Butler's come to town.

Some time ago they met before,
And started the Ball in Baltimore,
Ahoo!
When Polk and Dallas was the name,
But Cass and Butler's now the game.
Ahoo!
O' Cass and Butler's coming, coming, etc.

---

[1] *Lewis Cass eventually served as Secretary of State (1857-1860) under Buchanan. It is interesting to note that three other losing candidates also became Secretary of State after their parties came back into office: James G. Blaine (1889-1892), William Jennings Bryan (1913-1915), and Charles Evans Hughes (1921-1923). Henry Clay became Secretary of State under the man who defeated him (John Quincy Adams), and five men held this office at some time previous to their election to the Presidency: Thomas Jefferson (1789-1794), James Madison (1801-1809), James Monroe (1811-1817), John Quincy Adams (1817-1825), and James Buchanan (1845-1849).*

"OLD ROUGH AND READY"[1] 1848

President: *ZACHARY TAYLOR*

(1784-1850) of Virginia

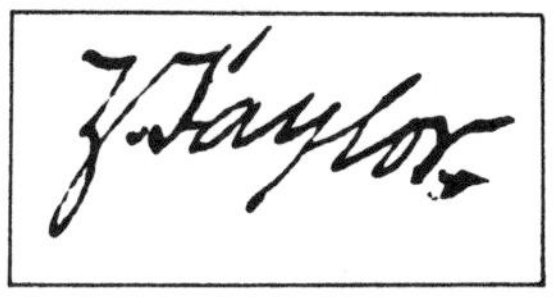

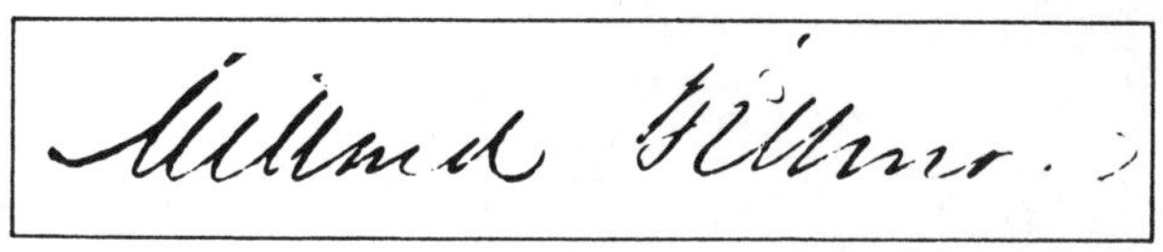

PREVIOUS OCCUPATIONS

State Legislature
Congressman
Lawyer
University President (Buffalo)
Vice President

Vice-President: Millard Fillmore[2]
Party: Whig
Convention: Philadelphia
Popular Vote: 1,360,101
Electoral Vote: 163

THE PLAINS OF MEXICO

"The Plains of Mexico" was not a Campaign Song but it is presented here because Taylor was one of the few presidents who became the subject of a popular folksong. The song deals with Taylor's heroics in the war with Mexico.

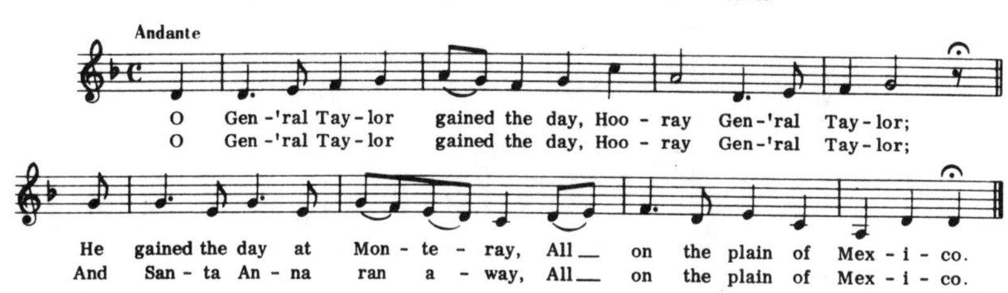

EXCERPT FROM INAUGURAL ADDRESS, MARCH 5, 1849:

". . . It is to be hoped that no international question can now arise which a government confident in its own strength and resolved to protect its own rights may not settle by wise negotiation; and it eminently becomes a government like our own, founded on the morality and intelligence of its citizens and upheld by their affections, to exhaust every resort of honorable diplomacy before appealing to arms . . ."

"FREE SOIL, FREE SPEECH, FREE LABOR, AND FREE MEN"

---

[1] "Rough and Ready" was Taylor's nickname. The "Free" slogan was neither Whig nor Democrat but was coined by a third party, "The Free-Soilers." Historians identify the 1848 campaign as "The Free-Soil Campaign." More information about the Free-Soilers and other third parties is contained in the appendix.

[2] July 9, 1850: Taylor dies and Vice-President Millard Fillmore becomes 13th President.

1852

Losing Candidate: WINFIELD SCOTT

(1786-1866) of Virginia

Running Mate: William A. Graham
Party: Whig[1]
Convention: Baltimore[2]
Popular Vote: 1,386,578
Electoral Vote: 42

OCCUPATIONS OF CANDIDATE

Lawyer
Army (General)
War of 1812
Blackhawk War
Seminole War
Mexican War
Civil War

"OLD FUSS AND FEATHERS"

GALLANT SCOTT IS OUR CHOICE

(Tune: The Star-Spangled Banner)

From the pine-covered hills, where dark Arostook flows,
To the gold-sanded shores blue Pacific is laving,
Where the Mexican cactus and wild dahlia grows,
Where o'er the broad prairie rich cornfields are waving,
Comes the glad pealing shout
Of bold freeman rung out --
While our proud flag is flung, in the welkin to float,
And the cannons proclaim, with their loud booming voice,
That the veteran in war, gallant SCOTT is our choice.

Then exultingly fling your proud flag to the breeze,
Inscribed WINFIELD SCOTT! a name famous in story;
And the motto we borrow from over the seas,
"We hope in God" yet, to emblazon with glory!
Success and applause,
To the gallant Whig cause,
To SCOTT and to GRAHAM, the UNION and LAWS!

---

[1] *With Winfield Scott's defeat, the Whig Party passed into the pages of history, never to resurface.*

[2] *Scott was nominated on the 53rd ballot.*

President: FRANKLIN PIERCE

1852

(1804-1869) of New Hampshire

"WE POLKED YOU IN '44, WE SHALL PIERCE YOU IN '52"

Vice-President: William R. King
Party: Democrat
Convention: Baltimore[1]
Popular Vote: 1,601,474
Electoral Vote: 252

DEMOCRATIC BATTLE-HYMN

Sturdy and strong we march along,
Millions on millions of freemen bold:
Rousing the dead with our iron tread--
The noble dead of the days of old!

Shadows they come, while the angry drum
And the trumpet fierce the war-note sound:
Calmly and solemn marching in column,
But noiseless their feet along the ground.

Heading the lines, where our standard shines,
A banner of fire to daunt the foe;
This sacred band, from the unknown land,
Has joined our ranks, as on we go.

Far in the van, like a living man,
Rides the kingly shade of a Hero gone,
The Chieftain-Sage of the Hermitage!
And his flaming sword waves -- On! march on!

He speaks--and along our serried throng
There is no sound but of tramping feet:
Like the hush of death is our silent breath;
Even our hearts forget to beat.

"Through the voiceless gloom of the silent tomb
Thundered your tread o'er the home of the dead!
Piercing the sod, like the voice of God!
Calling us hither to march at your head!

On! on to the field! and carved on your shield
As it burns on your banner, your battle-cry be,
For the People and God! so the trampled sod
Shall be the grand scene of your victory!
On! on now! march on! to die, but not yield!
For God and the People and Victory!"

On, brothers! march on! the field shall be won!
The dead and the living united are we!
Millions we come! while the angry drum
Sounds the grand march of victory!
For God and the People the battle shall be!
God and the People and Victory!

Washington, June 9th, 1852.

PREVIOUS OCCUPATIONS

Lawyer
State Legislature
Congressman
Senator
Army (Mexican War Brigadier General)

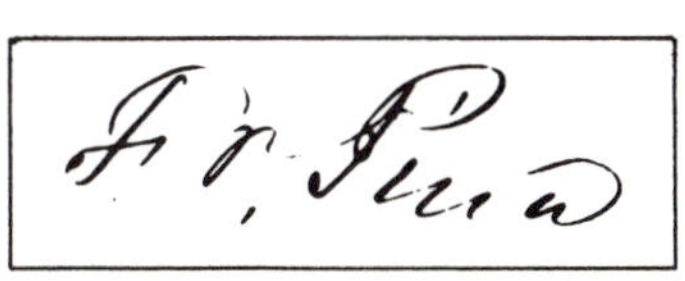

EXCERPT FROM INAUGURAL ADDRESS, MARCH 4, 1853:

". . . We have nothing in our history or position to invite aggression; we have everything to beckon us to the cultivation of relations of peace and amity with all nations. Purposes, therefore, at once just and pacific will be significantly marked in the conduct of our foreign affairs. I intend that my Administration shall leave no blot upon our fair record, and trust I may safely give the assurance that no act within the legitimate scope of my constitutional control will be tolerated on the part of any portion of our citizens which can not challenge a ready justification before the tribunal of the civilized world . . ."

[1] *Pierce was nominated on the 49th ballot.*

1856

Losing Candidate: JOHN C. FREMONT

(1813-1890) of Georgia

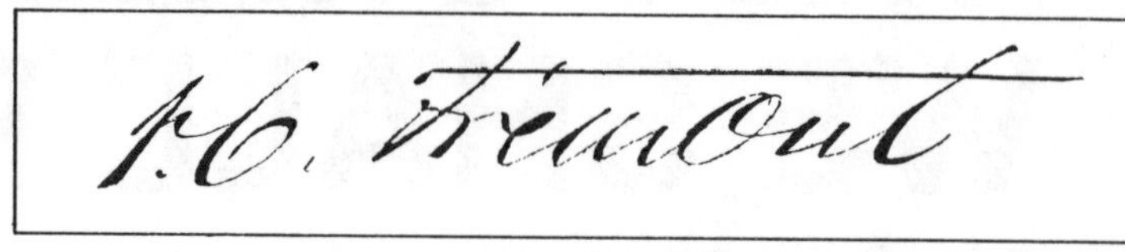

"FREE SPEECH, FREE PRESS, FREE SOIL, FREE MEN, FREMONT, AND VICTORY"

Running Mate: William L. Dayton
Party: Republican [1]
Convention: Philadelphia
Popular Vote: 1,335,264
Electoral Vote: 114

OCCUPATION OF CANDIDATE:
Professional soldier (General)

POLITICAL OFFICE HELD:
U. S. Senator from California

FREMONT'S BATTLE HYMN

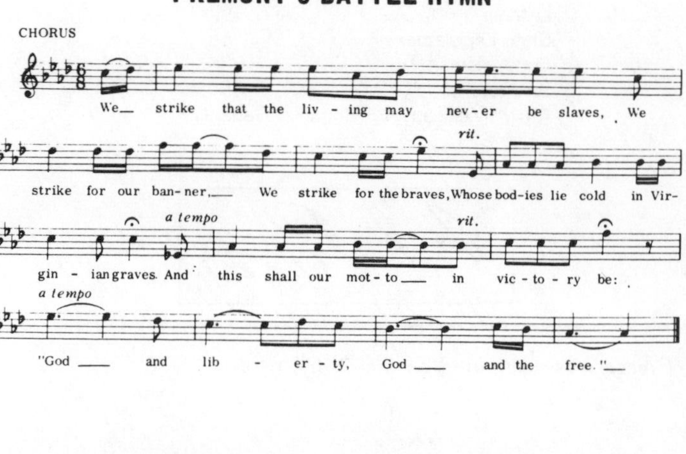

---

[1] *Differing opinions prevail among historians as to the location of the birth of the Republican Party. Credit for its founding has been given to both Ripon, Wisconsin, and Jackson, Michigan. In any case, the Republican Party was formed and named in 1854.*

President:
JAMES BUCHANAN
(1791-1868) of Pennsylvania
"OLD OBLIQUITY"

Vice-President: John C. Breckinridge
Party: Democrat
Convention: Cincinnati[1]
Popular Vote: 1,838,169
Electoral Vote: 174

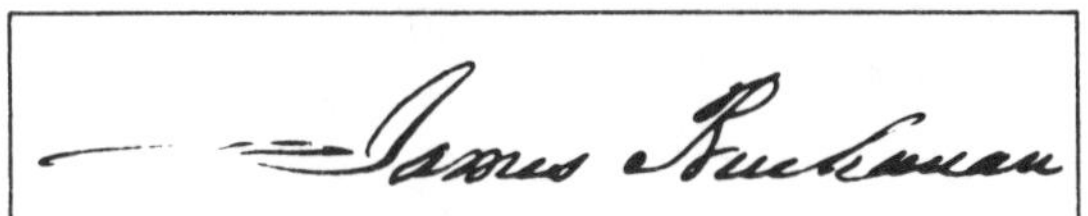

PREVIOUS OCCUPATIONS

Lawyer
Army (War of 1812)
State Legislature
Congressman
Ambassador (to Russia)
Senator
Secretary of State
Ambassador (to England)

EXCERPT FROM INAUGURAL ADDRESS, MARCH 4, 1857:

". . . It may be proper that on this occasion I should make some brief remarks in regard to our rights and duties as a member of the great family of nations. In our intercourse with them there are some plain principles, approved by our own experience, from which we should never depart. We ought to cultivate peace, commerce, and friendship with all nations, and this not merely as the best means of promoting our own material interests, but in a spirit of Christian benevolence toward our fellow-men, wherever their lot may be cast. Our diplomacy should be direct and frank, neither seeking to obtain more nor accepting less than is our due. We ought to cherish a sacred regard for the independence of all nations, and never attempt to interfere in the domestic concerns of any unless this shall be imperatively required by the great law of self-preservation . . ."

BUCHANAN'S UNION GRAND MARCH

In 19th century campaigns, "Grand Marches" were sometimes used instead of Campaign Songs. Here are the first few bars of one of many written for Buchanan.

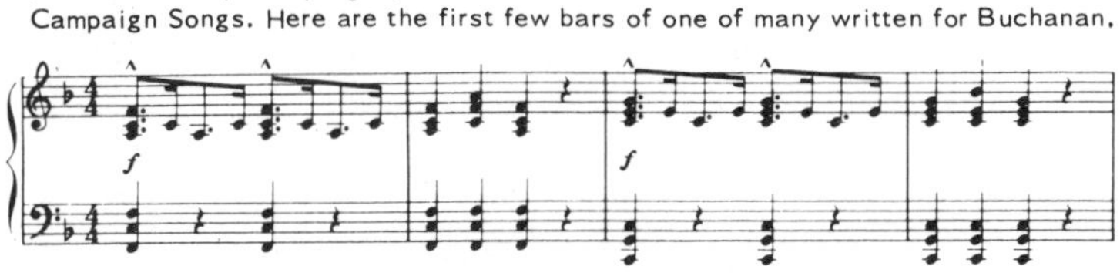

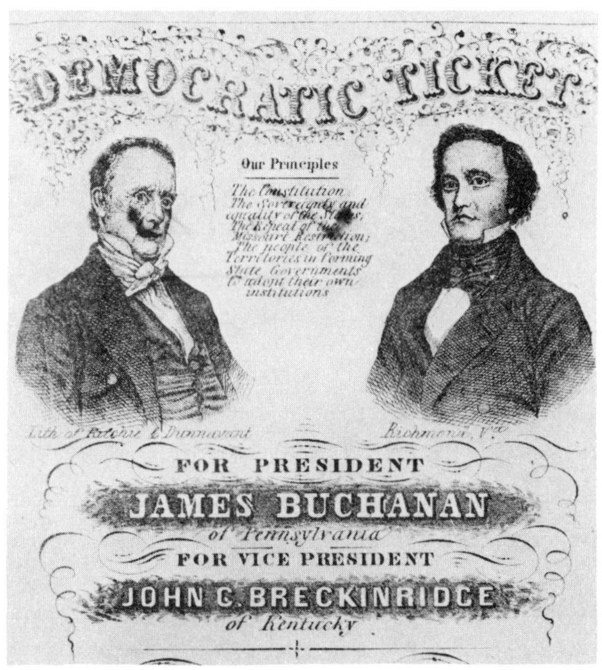

Detail of an 1856 Democratic ballot. [2]

[1] *Buchanan was nominated on the 17th ballot.*

[2] *The voters' mark which was scratched on the back of the ballot can be seen showing through the front between the two candidates' pictures.*

1860 "THE LITTLE GIANT"

Losing Candidate: STEPHEN A. DOUGLAS[1]

(1813-1861) of Vermont

Running Mate:
Benjamin Fitzpatrick
Party: Democrat
Convention:
Charleston & Baltimore[2]
Popular Vote: 1,375,157[3]
Electoral Vote: 12

OUR POLITICAL SNAKE-CHARMER.
DOUGLAS.—You perceive, ladies and gentlemen, that the creatures are entirely under my control. (Aside) Say, Forney, hope the brutes wont bite!

OCCUPATION OF CANDIDATE:
Lawyer, Politician

POLITICAL OFFICES HELD:
Illinois State Attorney
Illinois Secretary of State
Illinois Supreme Court Justice
U. S. House of Representatives
U. S. Senator (Illinois)

---

[1] *Although William Jennings Bryan is generally recognized as the first candidate to conduct a speech-making campaign tour in the modern fashion ("stumping"), it is Douglas who holds the distinction of being the first to "stump" for the presidency. Douglas however claimed that he was not soliciting votes, but speaking only to preserve the Union.*

[2] *The Charleston Convention lasted from April 23 to May 3; 57 ballots failed to produce a majority for any candidate so another convention was called in June at Baltimore during which Douglas was nominated on the second ballot.*

[3] *Douglas is usually considered Lincoln's chief opponent, but it should be noted that John C. Breckinridge (Democrat) had accumulated 845,763 popular and 72 electoral votes, and John Bell (Constitutional Union) received 598,581 popular and 39 electoral votes.*

1860

President:
ABRAHAM LINCOLN
(1809-1865) of Kentucky

Vice-President:
Hannibal Hamlin
Party: Republican
Convention: Chicago
Popular Vote: 1,866,252
Electoral Vote: 180

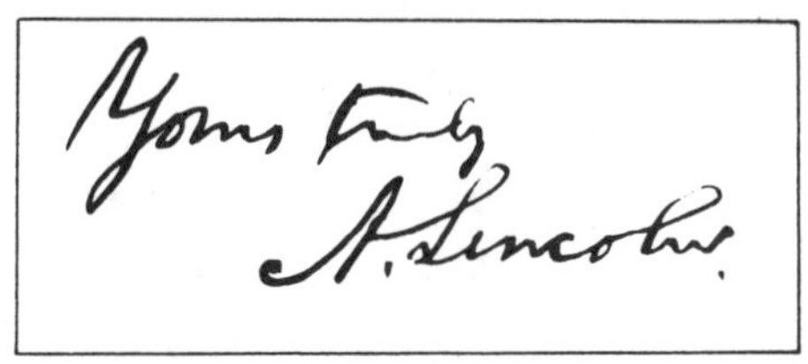

PREVIOUS OCCUPATIONS

Businessman
Army (Blackhawk War)
State Legislature (Whig Party: Illinios)
Lawyer
Congressman (Whig Party)

EXCERPT FROM 1st INAUGURAL ADDRESS, MARCH 4, 1861:

". . . In *your* hands, my dissatisfied fellow-countrymen, and not in *mine,* is the momentous issue of civil war. The government will not assail *you.* You can have no conflict without being yourselves the aggressors. *You* have no oath registered in Heaven to destroy the Government while *I* shall have the most solemn one to 'preserve, protect, and defend it.' . . ."

OLD ABE LINCOLN

(Tune: Old Grey Mare)

1864

Losing Candidate: GEORGE B. McCLELLAN

(1826-1885) of Pennsylvania

"PEACE AT ANY PRICE"

Running Mate: George H. Pendleton
Party: Democrat
Convention: Chicago
Popular Vote: 1,808,725
Electoral Vote: 21

OCCUPATION OF CANDIDATE:
Engineer and Professional Soldier (General)

POLITICAL OFFICES HELD:
(None)

McCLELLAN AND UNION

(Tune: Bonnie Dundee)

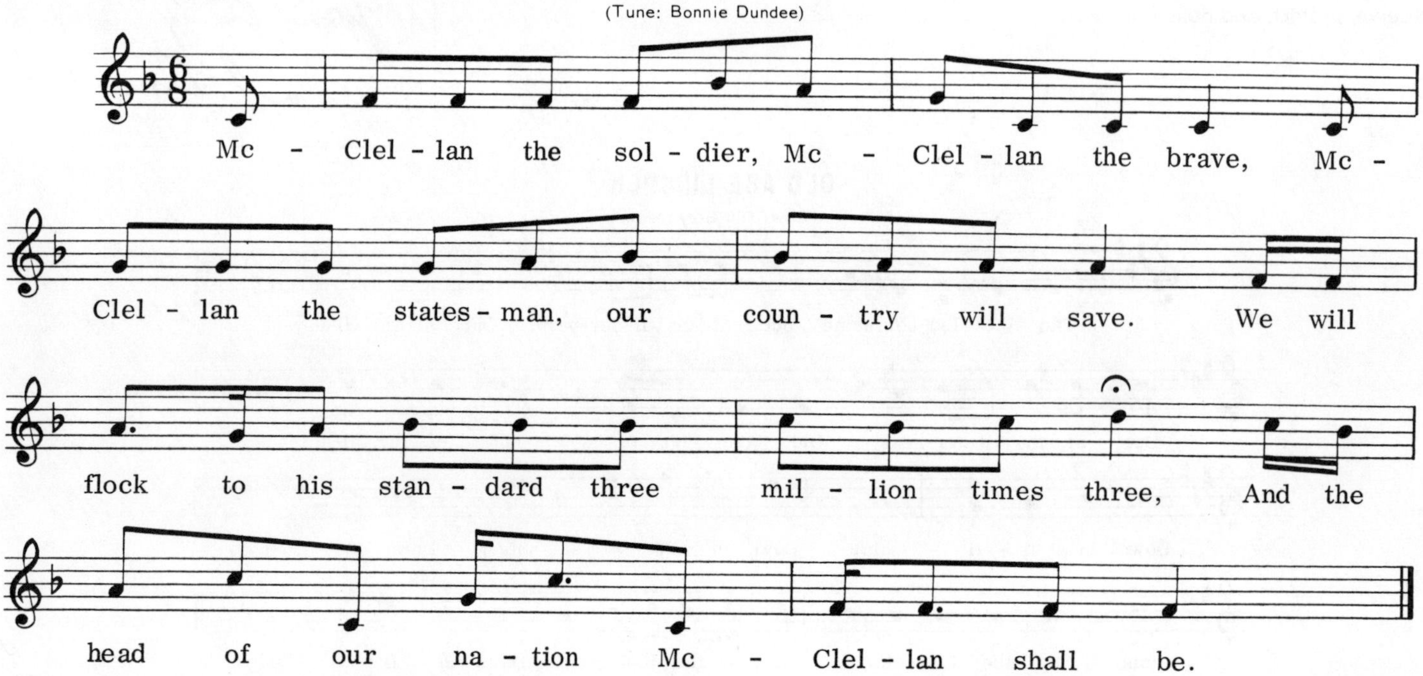

President: ABRAHAM LINCOLN

1864

"THE UNION FOREVER"

EXCERPT FROM 2nd INAUGURAL ADDRESS, MARCH 4, 1865:

". . . With malice toward none, with charity for all, with firmness in the right as God gives us to see the right, let us strive on to finish the work we are in, to bind up the nation's wounds, to care for him who shall have borne the battle and for his widow and his orphan, to do all which may achieve and cherish a just and lasting peace among ourselves and with all nations . . ."

PREVIOUS OCCUPATIONS

Tailor
Mayor (Greenville, Tennessee)
State Legislature
Congressman
Governor
Senator
Vice President

Vice-President:
Andrew Johnson[1],
Party: Republican[2]
Convention: Baltimore
Popular Vote: 2,216,067
Electoral Vote: 212

[1] *April 4, 1865: Lincoln is assassinated. He is succeeded by Andrew Johnson.*

[2] *The Republican Party appeared on the 1864 ballot as the National Union Party. See Third Party section for explanation.*

1868

Losing Candidate:

HORATIO SEYMOUR

(1810-1886) of New York

THE FIRST APPEARANCE OF THE DEMOCRATIC DONKEY

Drawn by Thomas Nast for the January 15, 1870 issue of Harper's Weekly.

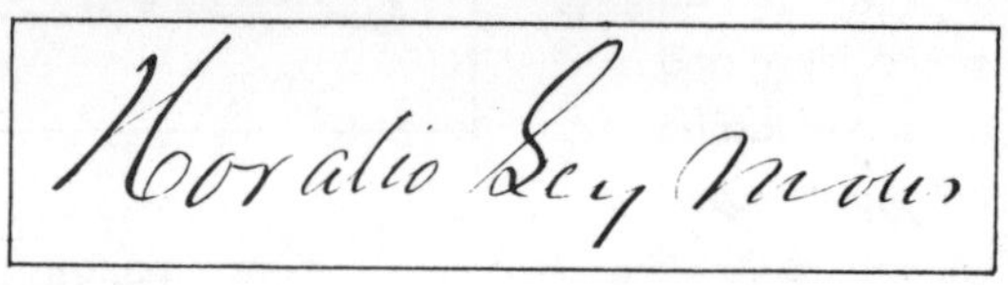

Running Mate: **Francis P. Blair**

Party: **Democrat**

Convention: **New York**[1]

Popular Vote: **2,709,615**

Electoral Vote: **80**

OCCUPATION OF CANDIDATE:
Lawyer, Politician

POLITICAL OFFICES HELD:
New York State Assembly
Mayor of Utica
Governor of New York

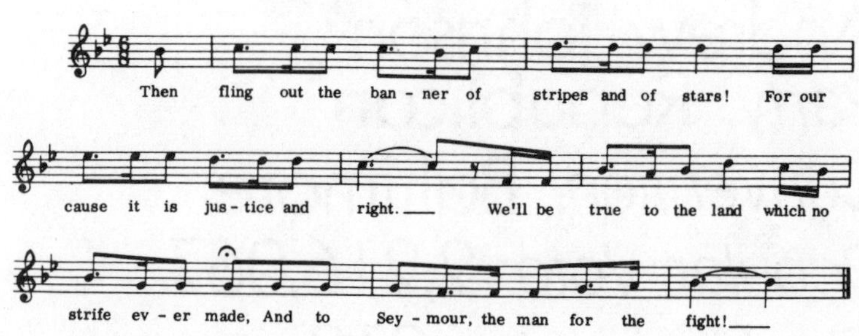

[1] *Seymour was the permanent president of the convention and not a candidate. After 21 ballots were taken, the leaders were Hancock and Hendricks. On the 22nd ballot Seymour's name appeared; during the ensuing "stampede" he resigned as convention president and was nominated on the 22nd ballot.*

1868

President: ULYSSES S. GRANT

(1822-1885) of Ohio

Vice-President: Schuyler Colfax

Party: Republican

Convention: Chicago

Popular Vote: 3,016,071

Electoral Vote: 214

EXCERPT FROM 1st INAUGURAL ADDRESS, MARCH 4, 1869:

". . . In regard to foreign policy, I would deal with nations as equitable law requires individuals to deal with each other, and I would protect the law-abiding citizen, whether of native or foreign birth, wherever his rights are jeopardized or the flag of our country floats. I would respect the rights of all nations, demanding equal respect for our own. If others depart from this rule in their dealings with us, we may be compelled to follow their precedent . . ."

PREVIOUS OCCUPATIONS

Army
Farmer
Businessman
General of the Army in Civil War

ULYSSES IS HIS NAME

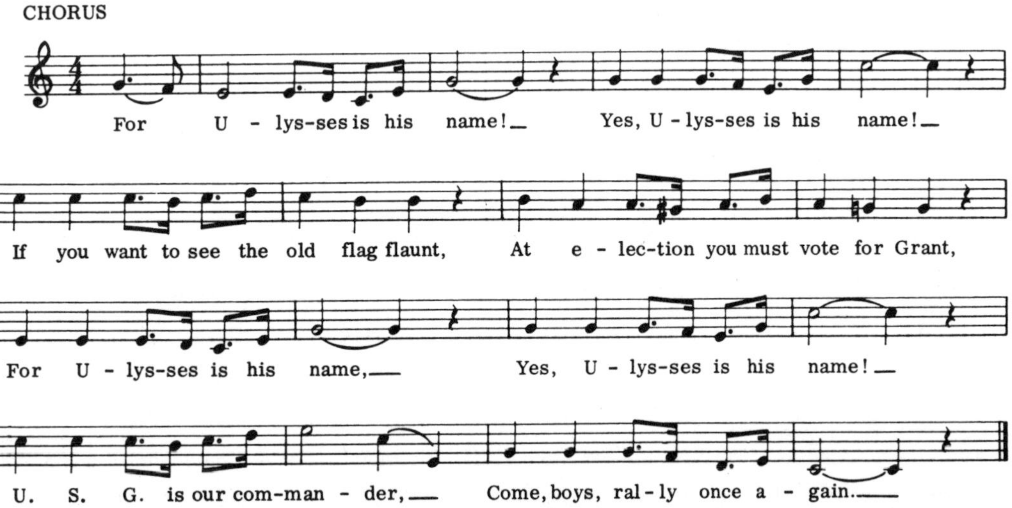

1872

Losing Candidate: *HORACE GREELEY*

(1811-1872) of New Hampshire

Running Mate:
B. Gratz Brown
Party: Democrat
Convention: Baltimore
Popular Vote: 2,834,079
Electoral Vote: 0[1]

OCCUPATION OF CANDIDATE:
Newspaper Publisher and Editor
POLITICAL OFFICE HELD:
U. S. House of Representatives

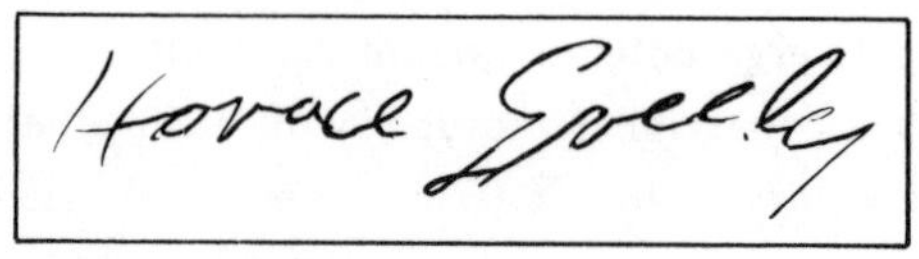

HORACE AND NO RELATIONS

This Campaign Song pointedly attacks one of the worst faults of the Grant Administration, excessive and blatant nepotism, as illustrated in the verse reproduced below the chorus.

Verse 3: Next their eyes so very wistful, Cast around to get a fist full Of the needful cash to fill their empty purses; And they fell on cheap relations, Who soon filled the public stations – Carpet-baggers, Uncles, Aunts, and e'en their Nurses.

---

[1] *Greeley had won 73 electoral votes, but since he died before the electors were chosen, his votes were dispersed among five minor candidates. The two men who received the majority of Greeley's votes were Thomas A. Hendricks (42) and B. Gratz Brown (18).*

President: ULYSSES S. GRANT

1872

Vice-President: Henry Wilson
Party: Republican
Convention: Philadelphia
Popular Vote: 3,597,070
Electoral Vote: 286

EXCERPT FROM 2nd INAUGURAL ADDRESS, MARCH 4, 1873:

". . . The effects of the late civil strife have been to free the slave and make him a citizen. Yet he is not possessed of the civil rights which citizenship should carry with it. This is wrong, and should be corrected. To this correction I stand committed, so far as Executive influence can avail . . ."

THE FIRST APPEARANCE OF THE REPUBLICAN ELEPHANT
Drawn by Thomas Nast for the November 7, 1874 issue of Harper's Weekly.

1876

"Losing"[1] Candidate: SAMUEL J. TILDEN

(1814-1886) of New York

Thomas A. Hendricks

OCCUPATION OF CANDIDATE:
Lawyer

POLITICAL OFFICES HELD:
New York State Legislature
Governor of New York

Advertisement appearing on back cover of one of the Tilden-Hendricks' campaign songs.

Running Mate: Thomas A. Hendricks
Party: Democrat
Convention: St. Louis
Popular Vote: 4,284,757
Electoral Vote: 184

PUT THE RIGHT MAN AT THE WHEEL

CHORUS

Will S. Hays

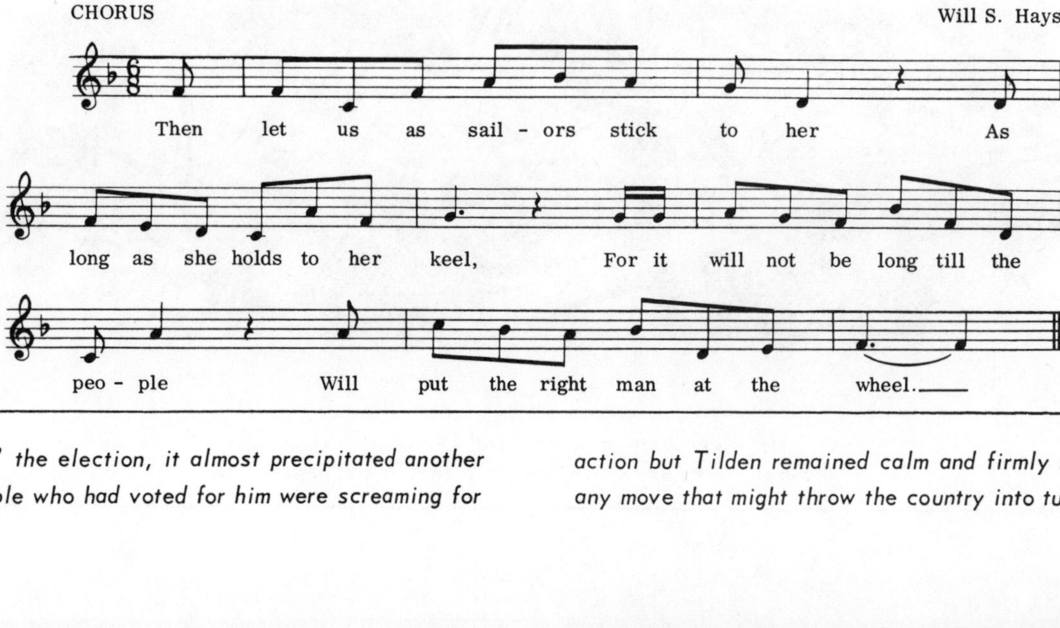

[1] *When Tilden "lost" the election, it almost precipitated another Civil War. The people who had voted for him were screaming for action but Tilden remained calm and firmly refused to sanction any move that might throw the country into turmoil.*

President: RUTHERFORD B. HAYES

(1822-1893) of Ohio

1876

PREVIOUS OCCUPATIONS
Lawyer
General (Civil War)
Congressman
Governor

Vice-President: William A. Wheeler
Party: Republican
Convention: Cincinnati
Popular Vote: 4,033,950
Electoral Vote: 185[1]

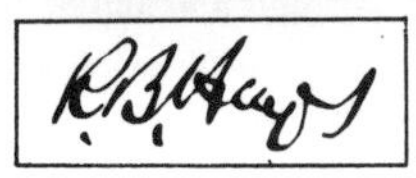

EXCERPT FROM INAUGURAL ADDRESS, MARCH 5, 1877:[2]

". . . at the basis of all prosperity, for that as well as for every other part of the country, lies the improvement of the intellectual and moral condition of the people. Universal suffrage should rest upon universal education. To this end, liberal and permanent provision should be made for the support of free schools by the State governments, and, if need be, supplemented by legitimate aid from national authority . . ."

HAYES THE TRUE AND WHEELER TOO

This song is the famous "Tippecanoe and Tyler Too" with new words. The song sheet anounces that it was arranged by R. E. Publican.

This cartoon by Thomas Nast describes the political situation of 1876 very well. The "Tiger" was also being used concurrently with the "Donkey" as a symbol of the Democratic Party.

---

[1] *Tilden had a clear plurality in the popular vote and the original electoral count was Tilden 184, Hayes 165, and 20 disputed votes. After much deliberation a committee of fifteen made up of Senators, Congressmen and Supreme Court Justices was formed to settle the dispute. Hayes was awarded the twenty disputed votes giving him 185 electoral votes and the Presidency. It is interesting to note that the above-mentioned committee was made up of eight Republicans and seven Democrats and that the members voted according to party affiliation.*

[2] *Perhaps the most deservedly famous line of Hayes' career occurred in his Inaugural Address: "He serves his Party best who serves his country best."*

1880

Losing Candidate: WINFIELD S. HANCOCK

(1824-1886) of Pennsylvania

Running Mate: William H. English
Party: Democrat
Convention: Cincinnati
Popular Vote: 4,442,030
Electoral Vote: 155

OCCUPATION OF CANDIDATE:
Professional Soldier (General)

WHEN HANCOCK TAKES THE CHAIR

This song was written by the composer of the famous "I'll Take You Home Again Kathleen," Thomas P. Westendorf.

President: JAMES A. GARFIELD (1831-1881) of Ohio

1880

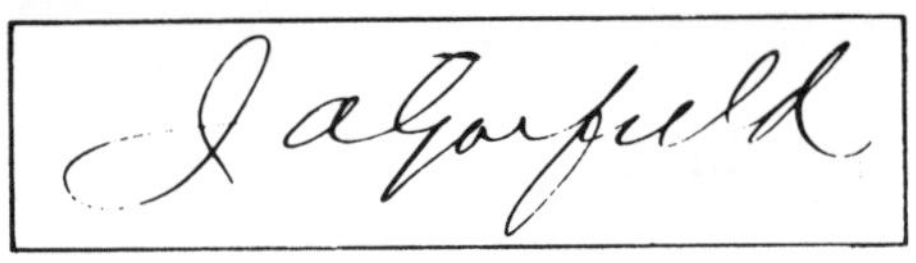

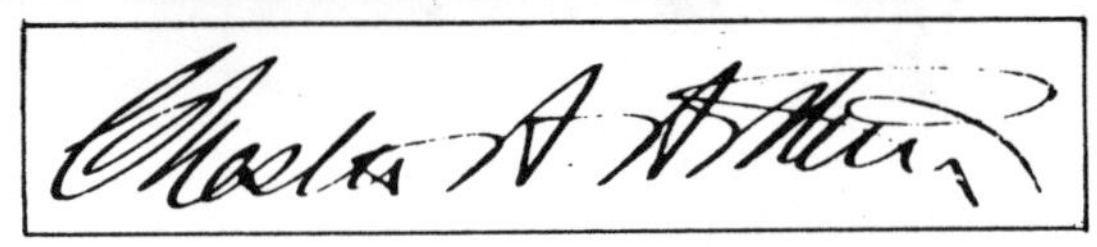

PREVIOUS OCCUPATIONS

College Teacher
General (Civil War)
Congressman (1863-1880)

HIS NAME IS GENERAL G

PREVIOUS OCCUPATIONS

School Teacher
Lawyer
Inspector General (New York Militia)
Collector (Port of New York)
Vice President

Vice-President: Chester A. Arthur[1]

Party: Republican

Convention: Chicago[2]

Popular Vote: 4,449,053

Electoral Vote: 214

EXCERPT FROM INAUGURAL ADDRESS, MARCH 4, 1881:

". . . The free enjoyment of equal suffrage is still in question, and a frank statement of the issue may aid its solution. It is alleged that in many communities negro citizens are practically denied the freedom of the ballot . . . . to violate the freedom and sanctities of the suffrage is more than an evil. It is a crime which, if persisted in, will destroy the Government itself. Suicide is not a remedy. If in other lands it be high treason to compass the death of the king, it shall be counted no less a crime here to strangle our sovereign power and stifle its voice . . ."

[1]*On July 2, 1881, President Garfield was shot by a disappointed office-seeker. Upon his death, September 19, 1881, Chester A. Arthur becomes the 21st president of the United States.*

[2]*Garfield was nominated on the 36th ballot. It is interesting to note that ex-president Grant (who had had two terms and was out of office for 4 years) led on the first 35 ballots and lost the final decisive 36th ballot by only 93 votes (Garfield 399, Grant 306).*

1884

Losing Candidate:
JAMES G. BLAINE
(1830-1893) of Pennsylvania

"THE PLUMED KNIGHT"

Running Mate: John A. Logan
Party: Republican
Convention: Chicago
Popular Vote: 4,848,334
Electoral Vote: 182

OCCUPATION OF CANDIDATE:
Lawyer, Teacher
Newspaper Editor, Politician

POLITICAL OFFICES HELD:
Maine State Legislature
U. S. House of Representatives
U. S. Senator (Maine)
Secretary of State

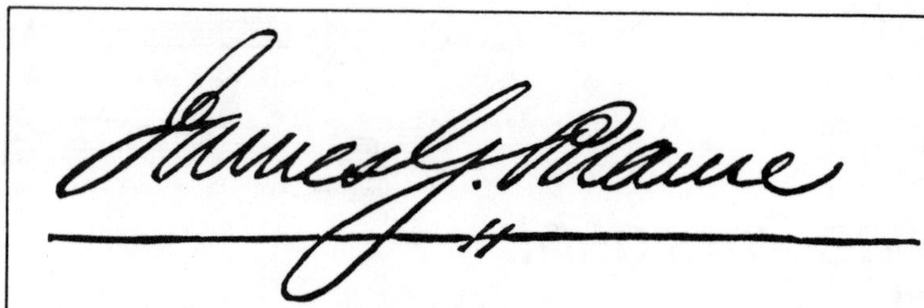

OUR PLUMED KNIGHT LEADS THE WAY

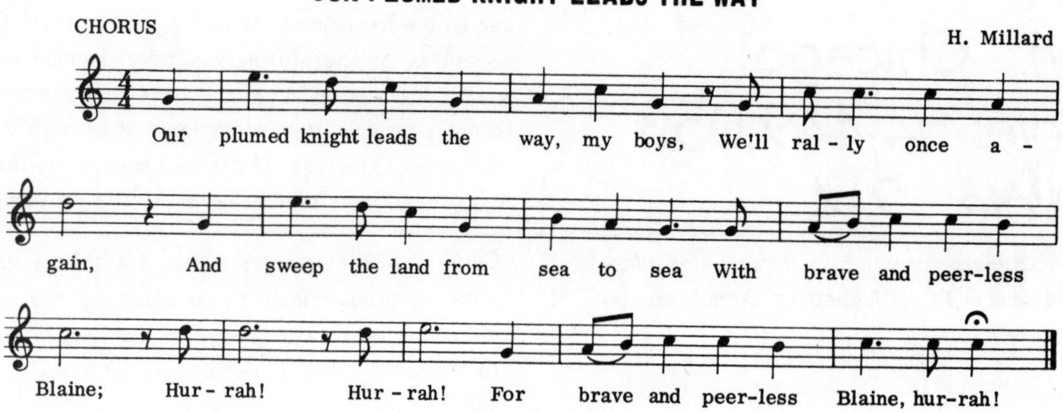

President: GROVER CLEVELAND

1884

(1837-1908) of New Jersey

Vice-President: Thomas A. Hendricks

Party: Democrat

Convention: Chicago

Popular Vote: 4,911,017

Electoral Vote: 219

The inauguration of President Cleveland.

PREVIOUS OCCUPATIONS

Lawyer
Sheriff (Erie County, N.Y.)
Mayor
Governor

EXCERPT FROM 1st INAUGURAL ADDRESS, MARCH 4, 1885:

". . . Today the executive branch of the government is transferred to new keeping. But this is still the government of all the people, and it should be none the less an object of their affectionate solicitude. At this hour the animosities of political strife, the bitterness of partisan defeat, and the exultation of partisan triumph should be supplanted by an ungrudging acquiescence in the popular will and a sober, conscientious concern for the general weal. Moreover, if from this hour we cheerfully and honestly abandon all sectional prejudice and distrust, and determine with manly confidence in one another, to work out harmoniously the achievement of our national destiny, we shall deserve to realize all the benefits which our happy form of government can bestow . . ."

CAMPAIGN JUBILEE SONG

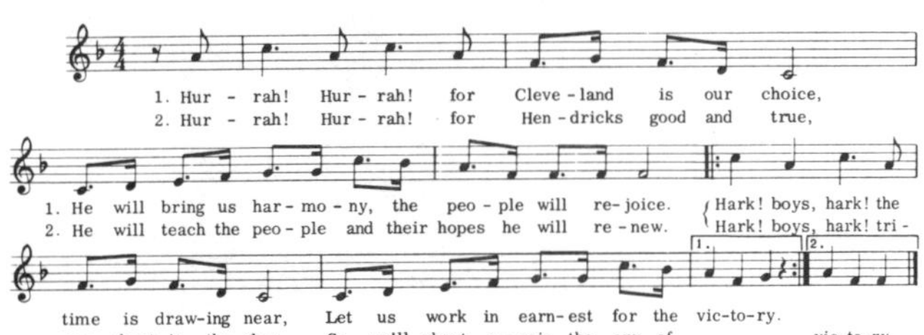

"BLAINE, BLAINE, JAMES G. BLAINE, CONTINENTAL LIAR FROM THE STATE OF MAINE"

1888

Losing Candidate: GROVER CLEVELAND

Running Mate: Allen G. Thurman
Party: Democrat
Convention: St. Louis
Popular Vote: 5,540,050
Electoral Vote: 168

STATE	POPULAR VOTE: Benjamin Harrison, Indiana	POPULAR VOTE: Grover Cleveland, New York	ELECTORAL VOTE: Harrison and Morton	ELECTORAL VOTE: Cleveland and Thurman
Alabama	56,197	117,320	–	10
Arkansas	58,752	85,962	–	7
California	124,816	117,729	8	–
Colorado	50,774	37,567	3	–
Connecticut	74,584	74,920	–	6
Delaware	12,973	16,414	–	3
Florida	26,657	39,561	–	4
Georgia	40,496	100,499	–	12
Illinois	370,473	348,278	22	–
Indiana	263,361	261,013	15	–
Iowa	211,598	179,887	13	–
Kansas	182,934	103,744	9	–
Kentucky	155,134	183,800	–	13
Louisiana	30,484	85,032	–	8
Maine	73,734	50,481	6	–
Maryland	99,986	106,168	–	8
Massachusetts	183,892	151,856	14	–
Michigan	236,370	213,459	13	–
Minnesota	142,492	104,385	7	–
Mississippi	30,096	85,471	–	9
Missouri	236,257	261,974	–	16
Nebraska	108,425	80,552	5	–
Nevada	7,229	5,362	3	–
New Hampshire	45,728	43,458	4	–
New Jersey	144,344	151,493	–	9
New York	648,759	635,757	36	–
North Carolina	134,784	147,902	–	11
Ohio	416,054	396,455	23	–
Oregon	33,291	26,522	3	–
Pennsylvania	526,091	446,633	30	–
Rhode Island	21,968	17,530	4	–
South Carolina	13,736	65,825	–	9
Tennessee	138,988	158,779	–	12
Texas	88,422	234,883	–	13
Vermont	45,192	16,785	4	–
Virginia	150,438	151,977	–	12
West Virginia	77,791	79,664	–	6
Wisconsin	176,553	155,232	11	–
Total	5,444,337	5,540,050	233	168

Lest it be thought that 1888 was a repetition of the 1876 election we present the totals from every state. It takes only a glance to see that, although Cleveland had more popular votes, he lost to Harrison in all the largest states. Thus did Harrison capture the majority of electoral votes.

President: BENJAMIN HARRISON

(1833-1901) of Ohio

1888

Vice-President: Levi P. Morton
Party: Republican
Convention: Chicago
Popular Vote: 5,444,337
Electoral Vote: 233

PREVIOUS OCCUPATIONS

Lawyer
General (Civil War)
U.S. Senate

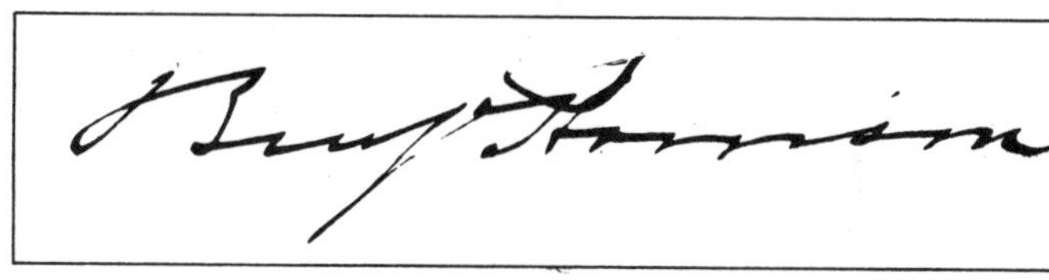

HIS GRANDFATHER'S HAT

(Tune: Grandfather's Clock)

This song is of course against the candidate but it reflects the unmerciful treatment that the opposition heaped upon him. Once Harrison was in office, the newspapers took up the theme of "His Grandfather's Hat" and Harrison took more pummeling.

Henry Clay Work

EXCERPT FROM INAUGURAL ADDRESS, MARCH 4, 1889:

". . . No other people have a government more worthy of their respect and love or a land so magnificent in extent, so pleasant to look upon, and so full of generous suggestion to enterprise and labor. God has placed upon our head a diadem and has laid at our feet power and wealth beyond definition or calculation. But we must not forget that we take these gifts upon the condition that justice and mercy shall hold the reigns of power and that the upward avenues of hope shall be free to all the people . . ."

1892

Losing Candidate: BENJAMIN HARRISON

Running Mate: Whitelaw Reid
Party: Republican
Convention: Minneapolis

Popular Vote: 5,190,802
Electoral Vote: 145

Joseph Keppler, co-publisher and cartoonist of the magazine "Puck," portrays Harrison as the character from Edgar Allan Poe's famous poem "The Raven." The raven is sitting on the bust of Harrison's grandfather (William Henry Harrison, 9th President) and Harrison sits dwarfed beneath his grandfather's hat. The cartoon is presented in deference to a more serious illustration as an example of the sometimes unmerciful criticism to which a candidate for the nation's highest office is subjected.

President: GROVER CLEVELAND

1892

Vice-President: Adlai E. Stevenson[1]

Party: Democrat
Convention: Chicago
Popular Vote: 5,554,414
Electoral Vote: 277

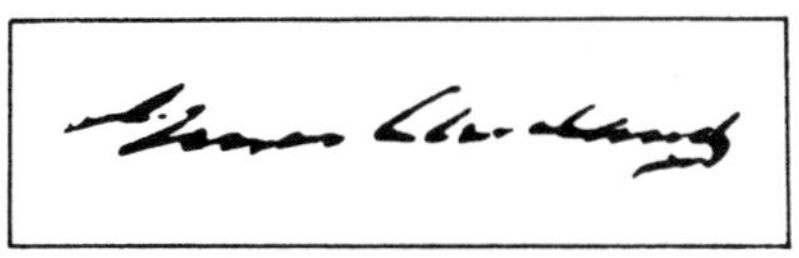

MUSIC COVERS
Reproduced here are the covers of three marches written for Cleveland's campaign.

EXCERPT FROM 2nd INAUGURAL ADDRESS, MARCH 4, 1893:

". . . Manifestly nothing is more vital to our supremacy as a nation and to the beneficent purposes of our Government than a sound and stable currency. Its exposure to degradation should at once arouse to activity the most enlightened statesmanship, and the danger of depreciation in the purchasing power of the wages paid to toil should furnish the strongest incentive to prompt and conservative precaution . . ."

---

[1] *Stevenson was the grandfather of Adlai E. Stevenson, the Democratic candidate of 1952 and 1956.*

1896

Losing Candidate: Wm. JENNINGS BRYAN[1]

(1860-1925) of Illinois

Running Mate: Arthur Sewell
Party: Democrat
Convention: Chicago
Popular Vote: 6,467,946
Electoral Vote: 176

HAVE YOU HEARD FROM MAINE?

(Tune: When Johnny Comes Marching Home Again)

This song, directed against Bryan, reflects the issue and mood of the time.

E. W. Locke

OCCUPATION OF CANDIDATE:
Lawyer, Newspaperman

POLITICAL OFFICES HELD:
U. S. House of Representatives
Secretary of State

"THE GREAT COMMONER"

EXCERPT FROM THE "CROSS OF GOLD" SPEECH:

". . . we will restore bimetallism, and then let England have bimetallism because the United States has it. If they dare to come out in the open field and defend the gold standard as a good thing, we will fight them to the uttermost. Having behind us the producing masses of this nation and the world, supported by the commercial interests, the laboring interests and the toilers everywhere, we will answer their demand for a gold standard by saying to them: You shall not press down upon the brow of labor this crown of thorns, you shall not crucify mankind upon a cross of gold . . ."

[1] *Bryan's first attempt to win the presidency was more exciting in several ways than his next two futile attempts. It was touched off by the famous "Cross of Gold" speech to the awed Chicago convention. He never again received so many electoral votes, and his influence with his party became little more than nominal by his third candidacy.*

"THE FRONT PORCH CAMPAIGN"[1] 1896

President: *WILLIAM McKINLEY*

(1843-1901) of Ohio

Vice-President: Garret A. Hobart
Party: Republican
Convention: St. Louis
Popular Vote: 7,035,638
Electoral Vote: 271

PREVIOUS OCCUPATIONS

Army (Civil War: Major)
Lawyer
Prosecuting Attorney
Congressman
Governor

EXCERPT FROM 1st INAUGURAL ADDRESS, MARCH 4, 1897:

". . . One of the lessons taught by the late election, which all can rejoice in, is that the citizens of the United States are both law-respecting and law-abiding people, not easily swerved from the path of patriotism and honor. This is in entire accord with the genius of our institutions, and but emphasizes the advantages of inculcating even a greater love for law and order in the future. Immunity should be granted to none who violate the laws, whether individuals, corporations, or communities . . ."

HURRAH FOR McKINLEY

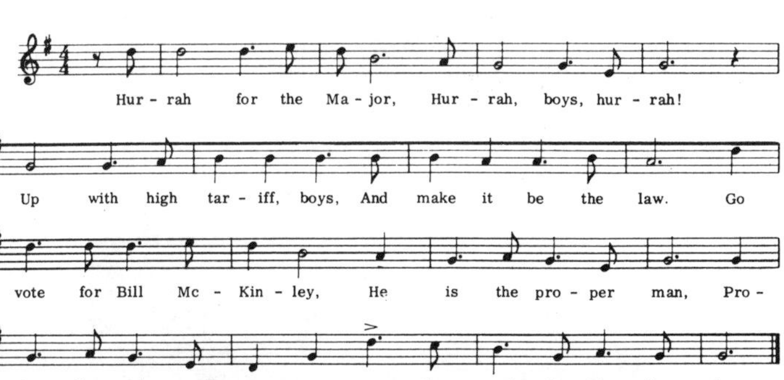

Chief Justice Fuller administering the oath of office to President-elect William McKinley.

[1] *While Bryan was barnstorming the entire country, sometimes delivering over a dozen speeches per day, McKinley received thousands of visitors while standing on his front porch in Canton, Ohio, throughout the campaign. After Bryan, all future Democratic candidates would "take to the stump."*

1900

Losing Candidate: Wm. JENNINGS BRYAN[1]

Running Mate: Adlai E. Stevenson
Party: Democrat
Convention: Kansas City
Popular Vote: 6,358,071
Electoral Vote: 155

THE VOTES IN THE 1900 ELECTION

STATES	POPULAR VOTE								ELECTORAL VOTE	
	McKinley and Roosevelt, Republican	Bryan and Stevenson, Democrat	Wooley and Metcalf, Prohibition	Debs and Harriman, Social-Democrat	Malloney and Remmel, Socialist-Labor	Barker and Donnelly, Mid-Road Populist	Ellis and Nicholson, Union Reform	Leonard and Martin, United Christian	McKinley and Roosevelt	Bryan and Stevenson
Alabama	55,512	97,131	2,762	—	—	4,178	—		—	11
Arkansas	44,800	81,142	584	27	—	972	341	—	—	8
California	164,755	124,985	5,087	7,572	—	—	—	—	9	—
Colorado	93,072	122,733	3,790	714	684	389	—	—	—	4
Connecticut	102,572	74,014	1,617	1,029	908	—	—	—	6	—
Delaware	22,535	18,863	546	57	—	—	—	—	3	—
Florida	7,420	28,007	2,234	601	—	1,070	—	—	—	4
Georgia	35,056	81,700	1,396	—	—	4,584	—	—	—	13
Idaho	27,198	29,414	857	—	—	232	—	—	—	3
Illinois	597,985	503,061	17,626	9,687	1,373	1,141	572	352	24	—
Indiana	336,063	309.584	13.718	2,374	663	1,438	254	—	15	—
Iowa	307,808	209,265	9,502	2,742	259	613	—	707	13	—
Kansas	185,955	162,601	3,605	1,605	—	—	—	—	10	—
Kentucky	226,801	234,899	2,814	770	299	2,017	—	—	—	13
Louisiana	14,233	53,671	—	—	—	—	—	—	—	8
Maine	65,412	36,822	2,585	878	—	—	—	—	6	—
Maryland	136,185	122,238	4,574	904	388	—	147	—	8	—
Massachusetts	239,147	157,016	6,208	9.716	2,610	—	—	—	15	—
Michigan	316,269	211.685	11,859	2,826	903	837	—	—	14	—
Minnesota	190,461	112,901	8,555	3,065	1,329	—	—	—	9	—
Mississippi	5,753	51,706	—	—	—	1,644	—	—	—	9
Missouri	314,092	351,922	5,965	6,139	1,294	4,244	—	—	—	17
Montana	25,373	37,145	298	708	169	—	—	—	—	3
Nebraska	121,835	114,013	3,655	823	—	1,104	—	—	8	—
Nevada	3,849	6,347	—	—	—	—	—	—	—	3
New Hampshire	54,799	35,489	1,279	790	—	—	—	—	4	—
New Jersey	221,754	164,879	7,190	4.611	2,081	691	—	—	10	—
New York	822,013	678,462	22,077	12,869	12,621	—	—	—	36	—
North Carolina	132,997	157,733	1,006	—	—	830	—	—	—	11
North Dakota	35,898	20,531	731	520	—	111	—	—	3	—
Ohio	543,918	474,882	10,203	4,847	1,588	251	4,284	—	23	—
Oregon	46,526	33,385	2,536	1,494	—	275	—	—	4	—
Pennsylvania	712,665	424,232	27,908	4,831	2,936	638	—	—	32	—
Rhode Island	33,784	19,812	1,529	—	1,423	—	—	—	4	—
South Carolina	3,579	47,233	—	—	—	—	—	—	—	9
South Dakota	54,530	39,544	1,542	169	—	339	—	—	4	—
Tennessee	123,180	145,356	3,860	413	—	1,322	—	—	—	12
Texas	130,641	267,432	2,644	1,846	162	20,981	—	—	—	15
Utah	47,139	45,006	209	720	106	—	—	—	3	—
Vermont	42,569	12,849	383	39	—	367	—	—	4	—
Virginia	115,865	146,080	2,150	145	167	63	—	—	—	12
Washington	57,456	44,833	2,363	2,066	866	—	—	—	4	—
West Virginia	119,829	98,807	1,692	219	—	268	—	—	6	—
Wisconsin	265,760	159,163	10,027	7,048	503	—	—	—	12	—
Wyoming	14,482	10,164	—	—	—	—	—	—	3	—
	7,219.525	6,358,737	209,157	94.864	33,432	50,599	5,698	1.059	292	155

[1] *In addition to his nickname "The Great Commoner," Bryan was called "The Boy Orator of the Platte" because he was only thirty-six in his first campaign. By his third campaign (1908) he was still younger than most presidential aspirants who had gone before him or would come after him.*

President: WILLIAM McKINLEY

1900

"FOUR MORE YEARS OF THE FULL DINNER PAIL"

Vice-President: Theodore Roosevelt[1]
Party: Republican
Convention: Philadelphia
Popular Vote: 7,219,530
Electoral Vote: 292

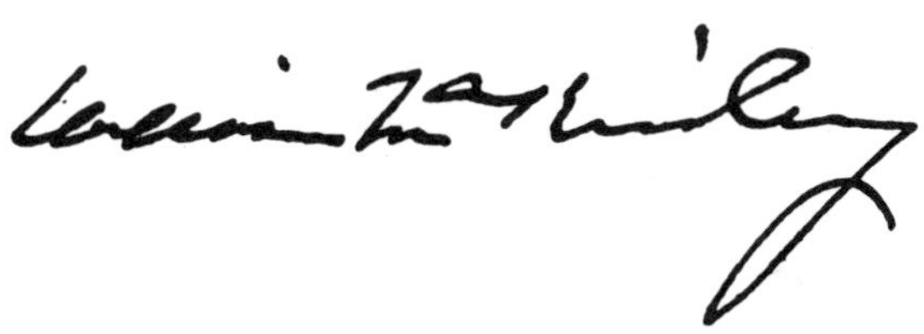

PREVIOUS OCCUPATIONS

Army (Civil War: Major)
Lawyer
Prosecuting Attorney
Congressman
Governor

EXCERPT FROM 2nd INAUGURAL ADDRESS, MARCH 4, 1901:

". . . The part which the United States bore so honorably in the thrilling scenes in China, while new to American life, has been in harmony with its true spirit and best traditions, and in dealing with the results its policy will be that of moderation and fairness.

"We face at this moment a most important question—that of the future relations of the United States and Cuba . . ."

[1] *William McKinley falls victim to an assassin's bullet, and he is succeeded by Theodore Roosevelt on September 14, 1901.*

1904

Losing Candidate: ALTON B. PARKER
(1852-1926) of New York

Running Mate: Henry G. Davis
Party: Democrat
Convention: Chicago
Popular Vote: 5,084,491
Electoral Vote: 140

OCCUPATION OF CANDIDATE:
Lawyer

POLITICAL OFFICES HELD:
Surrogate, Ulster County, N. Y.
Justice Supreme Court, N. Y.
Court of Appeals, N. Y.
Chief Justice, Court of Appeals, N. Y.

GOOD-BYE, TEDDY! YOU MUST MARCH! MARCH! MARCH!

"THE SQUARE DEAL" 1904

President:
THEODORE ROOSEVELT
(1858-1919) of New York

Vice-President: Charles W. Fairbanks

Party: Republican

Convention: Chicago

Popular Vote: 7,628,834

Electoral Vote: 336

PREVIOUS OCCUPATIONS

State Legislature
U.S. Civil Service
Commission Member
Police Commissioner of New York City
Assistant Secretary of Navy
Army Officer
Governor
Vice President

EXCERPT FROM INAUGURAL ADDRESS, MARCH 4, 1905:

". . . Our forefathers faced certain perils which we have outgrown. We now face other perils, the very existence of which it was impossible that they should foresee. Modern life is both complex and intense, and the tremendous changes wrought by the extraordinary industrial development of the last half century are felt in every fiber of our social and political being. Never before have men tried so vast and formidable an experiment as that of administering the affairs of a continent under the forms of a Democratic republic . . .

". . . There is no good reason why we should fear the future, but there is every reason why we should face it seriously, neither hiding from ourselves the gravity of the problems before us nor fearing to approach these problems with the unbending, unflinching purpose to solve them aright . . ."

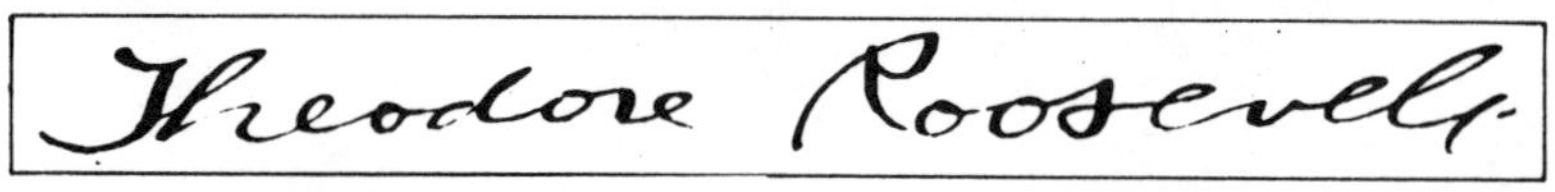

WE WANT TEDDY FOUR YEARS MORE

1908 Losing Candidate: Wm. JENNINGS BRYAN[1]

Running Mate: John W. Kern
Party: Democrat
Convention: Denver
Popular Vote: 6,409,106
Electoral Vote: 162

[1] *Bryan was finally rewarded for all his efforts when President Wilson appointed him Secretary of State in 1913. However, he resigned in 1915 because of a conflict of ideals and although he remained a fixture at Democratic conventions until 1924, his real political influence was ended.*

President: WILLIAM HOWARD TAFT

1908

(1857-1930) of Ohio

Vice-President: James S. Sherman

Party: Republican

Convention: Chicago

Popular Vote: 7,679,006

Electoral Vote: 321

PREVIOUS OCCUPATIONS

Superior Court Judge (Ohio)
U.S. Solicitor General
U.S. Circuit Court Judge
Governor (Philippine Islands)
Secretary of War
Chief Justice of The Supreme Court (after his Presidency: 1921-1930)

EXCERPT FROM INAUGURAL ADDRESS, MARCH 4, 1909:

". . . Our international policy is always to promote peace. We shall enter into any war with a full consciousness of the awful consequences that it always entails, whether successful or not, and we, of course, shall make every effort consistent with national honor and the highest national interest to avoid a resort to arms . . .

". . . In the international controversies that are likely to arise in the Orient growing out of the question of the open door and other issues the United States can maintain her interests intact and can secure respect for her just demands. She will not be able to do so, however, if it is understood that she never intends to back up her assertion of right and her defense of her interest by anything but mere verbal protest and diplomatic note . . ."

". . . The negroes are now Americans. Their ancestors came here years ago against their will, and this is their only country and their only flag. They have shown themselves anxious to live for it and to die for it. Encountering the race feeling against them, subjected at times to cruel injustice growing out of it, they may well have our profound sympathy and aid in the struggle they are making. We are charged with the sacred duty of making their path as smooth and easy as we can. Any recognition of their distinguished men, any appointment to office from among their number, is properly taken as an encouragement and an appreciation of their progress, and this just policy should be pursued when suitable occasion offers . . ."

GET IN LINE FOR BIG BILL TAFT

1912

Party: Progressive[1]

Losing Candidate: THEODORE ROOSEVELT

Running Mate: Hiram W. Johnson
Convention: Chicago
Popular Vote: 4,216,020
Electoral Vote: 88

Party: Republican[2]

Losing Candidate: WILLIAM HOWARD TAFT[3]

Running Mate: James S. Sherman
Convention: Chicago
Popular Vote: 3,483,922
Electoral Vote: 8

---

[1]*When Theodore Roosevelt bolted the Republican Convention he took some 300 delegates with him, attracted Senator LaFollette's Progressive followers, and formed the Bullmoose Party. The name was adopted because Roosevelt is supposed to have said he felt as fit as a bull-moose to plunge into the campaign.*

[2]*The split between Taft and Roosevelt was caused by several factors. First of all, the former President believed that Taft was not progressive enough. Secondly, he was influenced by unkind gossip about his old friend. Further, when a controversy developed between Gifford Pinchot (head of the U. S. Forest Service) and Richard Ballinger (Secretary of the Interior), Roosevelt was greatly displeased when Taft supported Ballinger.*

[3]*Nine years after his 1912 defeat Taft became the Chief Justice of the U. S. Supreme Court (appointed by President Harding) and served for nine years.*

1912

President: WOODROW WILSON
(1856-1924) of Virginia

Vice-President: Thomas R. Marshall
Party: Democrat
Convention: Baltimore[1]
Popular Vote: 6,286,214
Electoral Vote: 435

PREVIOUS OCCUPATIONS

College Teacher
University President (Princeton)
Governor (New Jersey)

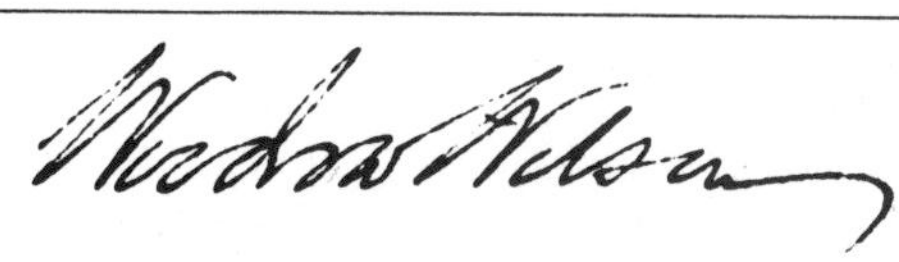

"THE NEW FREEDOM"

EXCERPT FROM 1st INAUGURAL ADDRESS, MARCH 4, 1913:

". . . There has been something crude and heartless and unfeeling in our haste to succeed and be great. Our thought has been "Let every man look out for himself, let every generation look out for itself," while we reared giant machinery which made it impossible that any but those who stood at the levers of control should have a chance to look out for themselves. We had not forgotten our morals. We remembered well enough that we had set up a policy which was meant to serve the humblest as well as the most powerful, with an eye single to the standards of justice and fair play, and remembered it with pride. But we were very heedless and in a hurry to be great . . ."

WILSON, THAT'S ALL

Ballard MacDonald — Geo. Walter Brown

CHORUS

From "WILSON, THAT'S ALL!" by Ballard MacDonald and George Walter Brown,
Copyright 1912 by Shapiro Music Publishing Co., New York, New York, used by permission

[1] *Wilson was nominated on the 46th ballot.*

1916

Losing Candidate:

CHARLES EVANS HUGHES

(1862-1948) of New York

Running Mate: Charles Warren Fairbanks
Party: Republican
Convention: Chicago
Popular Vote: 8,538,221
Electoral Vote: 254

OCCUPATION OF CANDIDATE:
Teacher, Lawyer

POLITICAL OFFICES HELD:
Governor of N. Y.
Associate Justice of U. S. Supreme Court
Secretary of State
Chief Justice, U. S. Supreme Court

President: WOODROW WILSON[1]

1916

Vice-President: Thomas R. Marshall
Party: Democrat
Convention: St. Louis
Popular Vote: 9,129,606
Electoral Vote: 277

"HE KEPT US OUT OF WAR"

I THINK WE'VE GOT ANOTHER WASHINGTON

EXCERPT FROM 2nd INAUGURAL ADDRESS, MARCH 5, 1917:

". . . The shadows that now lie dark upon our path will soon be dispelled and we shall walk with the light all about us if we be but true to ourselves—to ourselves as we have wished to be known in the counsels of the world and in the thought of all those who love liberty and justice and the right exalted."

---

[1] *During Wilson's second term the Nineteenth Amendment was ratified giving women the right to vote. The amendment states that "The right of citizens of the United States to vote shall not be denied or abridged by the United States or by any State on account of sex."*

1920

Losing Candidate:
JAMES M. COX
(1870-1957) of Ohio

Running Mate:
Franklin Delano Roosevelt[1]
Party: Democrat

Convention: San Francisco[2]
Popular Vote: 9,147,353
Electoral Vote: 127

OCCUPATION OF CANDIDATE:
Newspaper Publisher and Editor

POLITICAL OFFICES HELD:
U. S. House of Representatives
Governor of Ohio

[1]Franklin Delano Roosevelt has been the only candidate to run for Vice-President on a losing ticket and later become President.

[2]Cox was nominated on the 44th ballot.

President: WARREN G. HARDING
(1865-1923) of Ohio

1920

"THE SECOND FRONT PORCH CAMPAIGN"

Vice-President:
Calvin Coolidge[1]
Party: Republican
Convention: Chicago[2]
Popular Vote:
16,152,200
Electoral Vote: 404

PREVIOUS OCCUPATIONS

Newspaperman
State Legislature
Lieutenant Governor
Senator

LOYAL AMERICANS

March Song

EXCERPT FROM INAUGURAL ADDRESS, MARCH 4, 1921:

". . . America is ready to encourage, eager to initiate, anxious to participate in any seemly program likely to lessen the probability of war, and promote that brotherhood of mankind which must be God's highest conception of human relationship. Because we cherish ideals of justice and peace, because we appraise international comity and helpful relationship no less highly than any people of the world, we aspire to a high place in the moral leadership of civilization, and we hold a maintained America, the proven Republic, the unshaken temple of representative democracy, to be not only an inspiration and example, but the highest agency of strengthening good will and promoting accord on both continents . . ."

[1] *On Harding's death (August 2, 1923), Calvin Coolidge is sworn in as the 30th President by his father, a Justice of the Peace.*

[2] *Harding was nominated on the 10th ballot.*

1924

Losing Candidate: JOHN W. DAVIS

(1873-1955) of West Virginia

Running Mate: Charles W. Bryan[1]
Party: Democrat
Convention: New York City[2]
Popular Vote: 8,385,586
Electoral Vote: 136

OCCUPATION OF CANDIDATE:
Lawyer

POLITICAL OFFICES HELD:
U. S. House of Representatives
U. S. Solicitor General
Ambassador to Great Britain

MARCH TO THE WHITE HOUSE

[1] *Charles W. Bryan, Governor of Nebraska, was the brother of William Jennings Bryan.*

[2] *Davis was nominated on the 103rd ballot.*

President: CALVIN COOLIDGE

(1872-1933) of Vermont

1924

Vice-President: Charles G. Dawes

Party: Republican

Convention: Cleveland

Popular Vote: 15,725,016

Electoral Vote: 382

EXCERPT FROM INAUGURAL ADDRESS, MARCH 4, 1925:

". . . We have not failed, nor shall we fail to respond, whenever necessary to mitigate human suffering and assist in the rehabilitation of distressed nations. These, too, are requirements which must be met by reason of our vast powers and the place we hold in the world . . ."

PREVIOUS OCCUPATIONS

State Legislature (Mass.)
Lieutenant Governor (Mass.)
Mayor
Governor (Mass.)
Vice President

"SILENT CAL"

KEEP COOL AND KEEP COOLIDGE

1928

Losing Candidate: ALFRED E. SMITH

(1873-1944) of New York

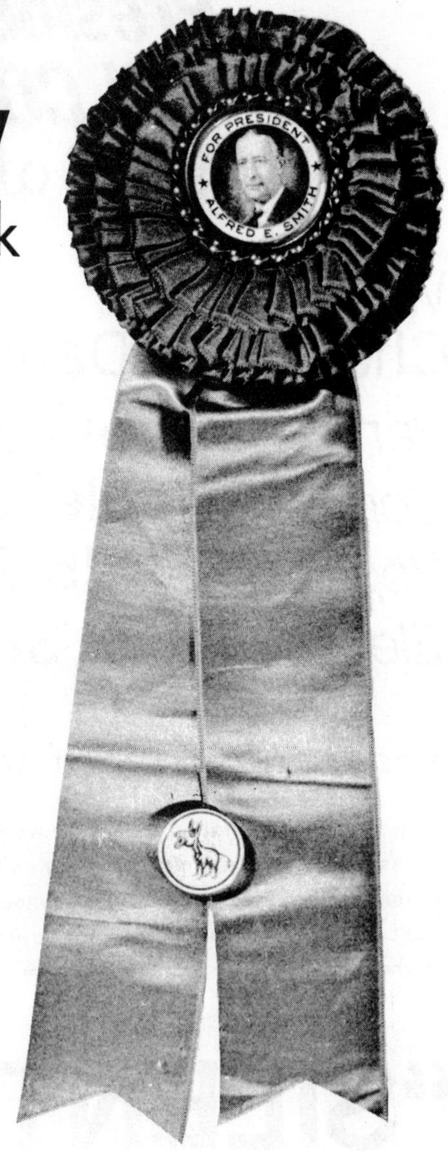

OCCUPATION OF CANDIDATE:
Politician

POLITICAL OFFICES HELD:
N. Y. State Assembly
Sheriff of N. Y. County
Governor of N. Y. State

THE SIDEWALKS OF NEW YORK

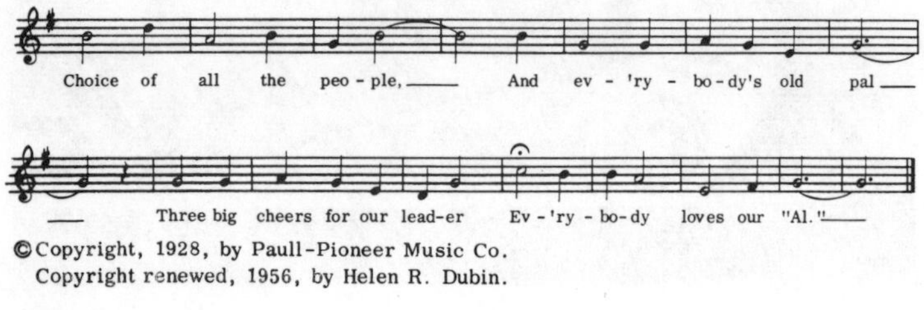

©Copyright, 1928, by Paull-Pioneer Music Co.
Copyright renewed, 1956, by Helen R. Dubin.

Running Mate:
Joseph T. Robinson

Party: Democrat

Convention: Houston

Popular Vote: 15,016,443

Electoral Vote: 87

President: HERBERT HOOVER[1] 1928

(1874-1964) of Iowa

Vice-President: Charles Curtis

Party: Republican

Convention: Kansas City, Mo.

Popular Vote: 21,392,190

Electoral Vote: 444

"A CHICKEN IN EVERY POT"

HOOVER RALLY SONG

PREVIOUS OCCUPATIONS

Mining Engineer
Secretary of Commerce

EXCERPT FROM INAUGURAL ADDRESS, MARCH 4, 1929:

". . . Although education is primarily a responsibility of the States and local communities, and rightly so, yet the Nation as a whole is vitally concerned in its development everywhere to the highest standards and to complete universality. Self-government can succeed only through an instructed electorate . . ."

[1] *Herbert Hoover was the only man elected to the Presidency who had held the office of Secretary of Commerce (1921-1923).*

1932

Losing Candidate:
HERBERT HOOVER

Running Mate: :
Charles Curtis
Party: Republican

Convention: Chicago
Popular Vote: 15,761,841
Electoral Vote: 59

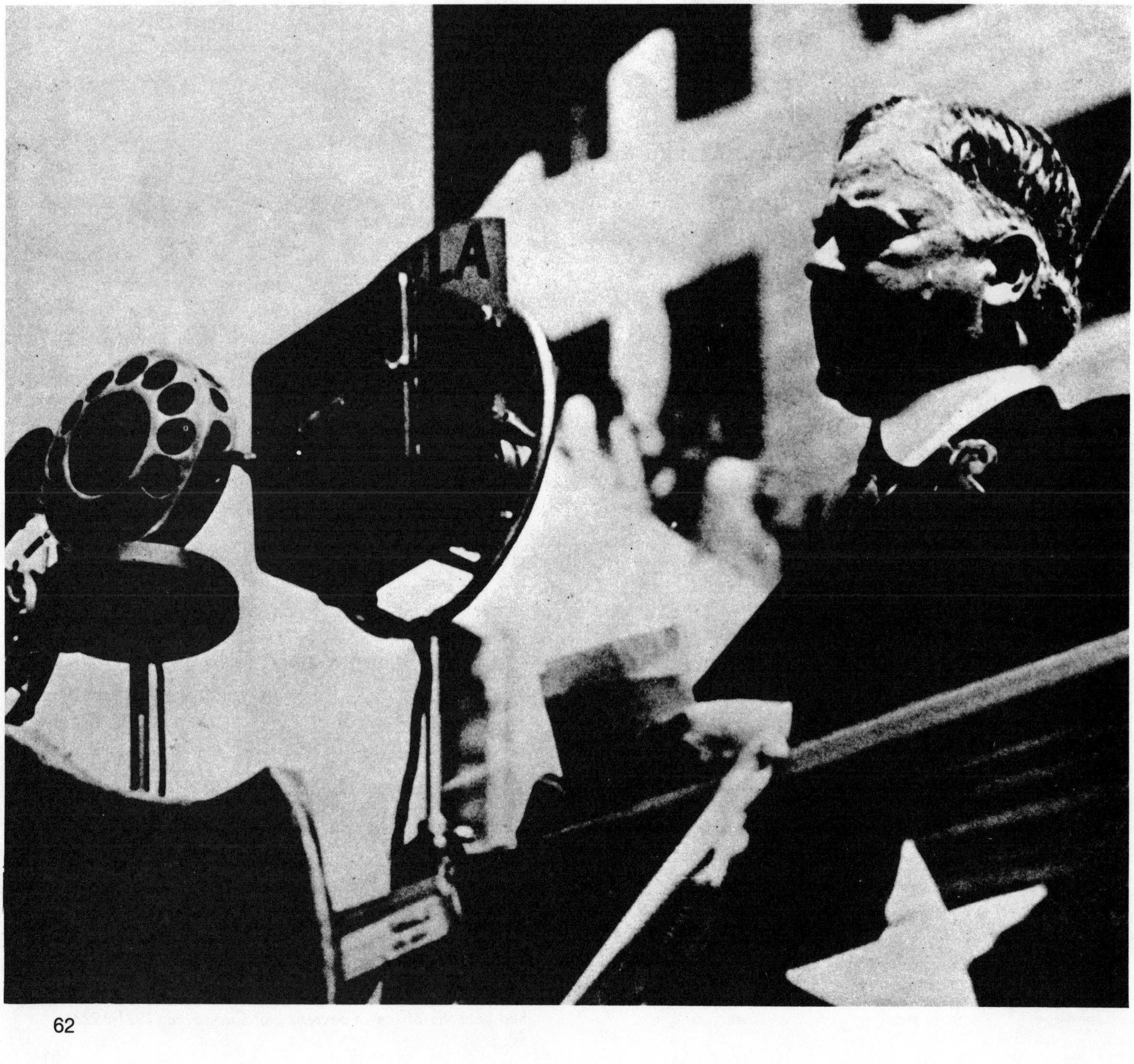

President: 1932
FRANKLIN DELANO ROOSEVELT
(1882-1945) of New York

Vice-President: John N. Garner
Party: Democrat

Convention: Chicago[1]
Popular Vote: 22,821,857
Electoral Vote: 472

"THE NEW DEAL"

EXCERPT FROM 1st INAUGURAL ADDRESS, MARCH 4, 1933:

". . . Happiness lies not in the mere possession of money; it lies in the joy of achievement, in the thrill of creative effort. The joy and moral stimulation of work no longer must be forgotten in the mad chase of evanescent profits. These dark days will be worth all they cost us if they teach us that our true destiny is not to be ministered unto but to minister to ourselves and to our fellow men . . ."

---

[1] *Franklin Delano Roosevelt broke with tradition immediately. He became the first nominee to make his acceptance speech at the convention, thus setting a precedent which has been followed by subsequent nominees of both parties.*

1936

Losing Candidate: ALFRED LANDON

(1887-) of Pennsylvania

"OFF THE ROCKS WITH LANDON AND KNOX"

Running Mate: Frank Knox
Party: Republican
Convention: Cleveland
Popular Vote: 16,679,583[1]
Electoral Vote: 8

OCCUPATION OF CANDIDATE:
Oilman

POLITICAL OFFICE HELD:
Governor of Kansas

LET'S LAND LANDON IN THE WHITE HOUSE

Thomas R. Johnstone — A. Maloof

[1] When Roosevelt's superb campaign manager Jim Farley predicted that the Democrats would carry every state but Maine and Vermont he aroused shouts of disbelief throughout the country. After the election Farley was joined by the disbelievers in adding a new twist to the time honored, if not altogether true, slogan "As Maine goes, so goes the Nation"; it now became "As Maine goes, so goes Vermont."

1936

President: FRANKLIN DELANO ROOSEVELT

Vice-President:
John N. Garner
Party: Democrat
Convention: Philadelphia[1]
Popular Vote: 27,751,597
Electoral Vote: 523

EXCERPT FROM 2nd INAUGURAL ADDRESS, JANUARY 20, 1937:

". . . I see one-third of a nation ill-housed, ill-clad, ill-nourished.

"It is not in despair that I paint you that picture. I paint it for you in hope—because the Nation, seeing and understanding the injustice in it, proposes to paint it out. We are determined to make every American citizen the subject of his country's interest and concern; and we will never regard any faithful law-abiding group within our borders as superfluous. The test of our progress is not whether we add more to the abundance of those who have much; it is whether we provide enough for those who have too little . . ."

---

[1] Until 1936 a two-thirds vote was necessary to nominate a Democratic candidate but, because of the new-found Democratic power in the large northern cities, the Convention was able to install the majority vote for this and all succeeding conventions. The Republican Party has used the majority vote system since its first convention in 1856.

CHORUS(excerpt) **ON WITH ROOSEVELT [2]**

[2] Many times in the past a current popular song became identified with a presidential candidate, sometimes to the exclusion of songs specifically written for the campaign. For example, "Happy Days Are Here Again" became "F.D.R.'s Song," to the exclusion of "On With Roosevelt." Another example is Teddy Roosevelt's "There'll Be a Hot Time in the Old Town Tonight." More recently "I Like Ike" from "Call Me Madam" was used by the Eisenhower campaigners, and in 1964 the Lyndon Johnson supporters paraphrased the title song of the popular "Hello, Dolly" to "Hello, Lyndon."

1940

OCCUPATION OF CANDIDATE:
Lawyer, Corporation Executive
POLITICAL OFFICES HELD:
None

Losing Candidate: *WENDELL WILLKIE*
(1892-1944) of Indiana

Running Mate:
Charles L. McNary
Party: Republican
Convention: Philadelphia
Popular Vote: 22,304,755
Electoral Vote: 82

1940

President:
FRANKLIN DELANO ROOSEVELT

Vice-President:
Henry A. Wallace
Party: Democrat
Convention: Chicago
Popular Vote: 27,243,466
Electoral Vote: 449

PREVIOUS OCCUPATIONS
State Legislature
Assistant Secretary of the Navy
Businessman
Governor

EXCERPT FROM 3rd INAUGURAL ADDRESS, JANUARY 20, 1941:

". . . A nation, like a person, has a body—a body that must be fed and clothed and housed, invigorated and rested, in a manner that measures up to the objectives of our time.

"A nation, like a person, has a mind—a mind that must be kept informed and alert, that must know itself, that understands the hopes and the needs of its neighbors—all the other nations that live within the narrowing circle of the world.

"And a nation, like a person, has something deeper, something more permanent, something larger than the sum of all its parts. It is that something which matters most to its future—which calls forth the most sacred guarding of its present . . ."

1944

Losing Candidate:
THOMAS E. DEWEY
(1902-1971) of Michigan

Running Mate:
John W. Bricker
Party: Republican
Convention: Chicago
Popular Vote: 22,006,278
Electoral Vote: 99

OCCUPATION OF CANDIDATE:
Lawyer

POLITICAL OFFICES HELD:
U. S. Attorney for Southern District of N. Y.
District Attorney, N. Y.
Governor of New York

1944

President:
FRANKLIN DELANO ROOSEVELT

Vice-President:
Harry S. Truman[1]
Party: Democrat
Convention: Chicago
Popular Vote: 25,602,505
Electoral Vote: 432

EXCERPT FROM 4th INAUGURAL ADDRESS, JANUARY 20, 1945:

". . . We have learned that we cannot live alone, at peace; that our own well-being is dependent on the well-being of other nations far away. We have learned that we must live as men, not as ostriches, nor as dogs in the manger.

"We have learned to be citizens of the world, members of the human community.

"We have learned the simple truth, as Emerson said, that 'The only way to have a friend is to be one.'

"We can gain no lasting peace if we approach it with suspicion and mistrust or with fear. We can gain it only if we proceed with the understanding, the confidence, and the courage which flow from conviction. . ."

---

[1] *On the death of Franklin D. Roosevelt, April 12, 1945, Harry S. Truman becomes the 33rd President.*

Due to the ratification of the Twenty-Second Amendment during President Truman's administration, no president since Roosevelt has been legally permitted to seek a third term. The amendment reads in part: "No person shall be elected to the office of the President more than twice . . ."

1948

Losing Candidate:
THOMAS E. DEWEY

Running Mate: Earl Warren
Party: Republican

Convention: Philadelphia
Popular Vote: 21,970,065
Electoral Vote: 189

TOM DEWEY FOR PRESIDENT

Words and Music by
Roslyn Wells (Addison)

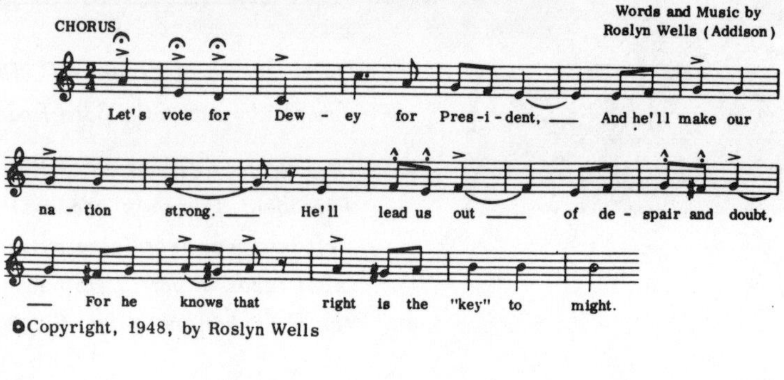

©Copyright, 1948, by Roslyn Wells

"THE FAIR DEAL" 1948

President: HARRY S. TRUMAN

(1884-1972)of Missouri

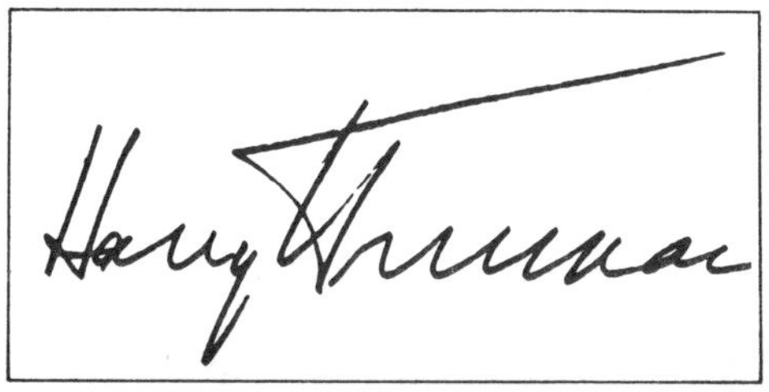

PREVIOUS OCCUPATIONS

Army (WW1)
Businessman
Judge
Senator
Vice President

Vice-President:

Alben W. Barkley
Party: Democrat
Convention: Philadelphia
Popular Vote: 24,105,812[1]
Electoral Vote: 303

EXCERPT FROM INAUGURAL ADDRESS, JANUARY 20, 1949:

". . . It may be our lot to experience, and in a large measure to bring about, a major turning point in the long history of the human race. The first half of this century has been marked by unprecedented and brutal attacks on the rights of man, and by the two most frightful wars in history. The supreme need of our time is for men to learn to live together in peace and harmony.

"The peoples of the earth face the future with grave uncertainty, composed almost equally of great hopes and great fears. In this time of doubt, they will look to the United States as never before for good will, strength, and wise leadership . . ."

[1] *It is not generally known that there was one pollster who did not predict victory for Dewey. This solitary prophet was Louis Bean.*

1952

Losing Candidate:
ADLAI E. STEVENSON
(1900-1965) of California

OCCUPATION OF CANDIDATE:
Lawyer
POLITICAL OFFICES HELD:
Governor of Illinois
U. S. Ambassador to the U.N.

Running Mate:
John J. Sparkman
Party: Democrat
Convention: Chicago
Popular Vote: 27,314,992
Electoral Vote: 89

President: DWIGHT D. EISENHOWER

1952

(1890-1969) of Texas

Vice-President: Richard M. Nixon
Party: Republican
Convention: Chicago
Popular Vote: 33,936,252
Electoral Vote: 442

PREVIOUS OCCUPATIONS
Army (WW1 & WW2) (Five Star General)
University President (Columbia)

EXCERPT FROM 1st INAUGURAL ADDRESS, JANUARY 20, 1953:

". . . Conceiving the defense of freedom, like freedom itself, to be one and indivisible, we hold all continents and peoples in equal regard and honor. We reject any insinuation that one race or another, one people or another, is in any sense inferior or expendable.

"Respecting the United Nations as the living sign of all people's hope for peace, we shall strive to make it not merely an eloquent symbol but an effective force. And in our quest for an honorable peace, we shall neither compromise, nor tire, nor ever cease . . ."

I LIKE IKE
(First 16 Bars)

Words and Music by Irving Berlin

© Copyright, 1950, by IRVING BERLIN
Copyright, 1952, by IRVING BERLIN
Reprinted by permission of Irving Berlin Music Corporation.

1956

Losing Candidate: ADLAI E. STEVENSON

Running Mate: Estes Kefauver
Party: Democrat
Convention: Chicago
Popular Vote: 26,031,322
Electoral Vote: 73

Words by
Anne Croswell

BELIEVE IN STEVENSON

Music by
Ed Scott

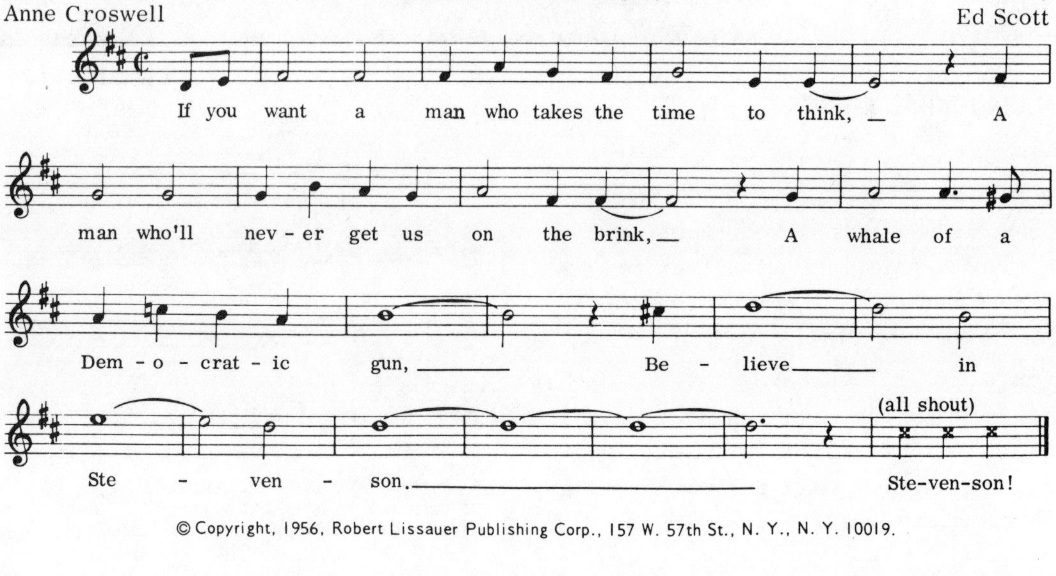

© Copyright, 1956, Robert Lissauer Publishing Corp., 157 W. 57th St., N. Y., N. Y. 10019.

President: DWIGHT D. EISENHOWER[1]

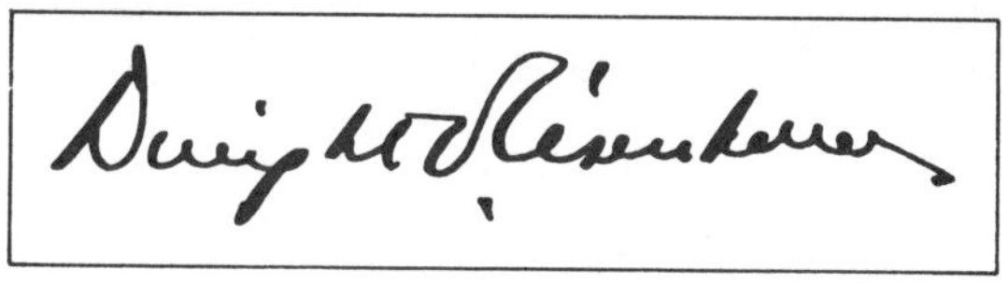

Vice-President: Richard M. Nixon
Party: Republican
Convention: San Francisco
Popular Vote: 35,585,316
Electoral Vote: 457

EXCERPT FROM 2nd INAUGURAL ADDRESS, JANUARY 20,1957:

". . . We cherish our friendship with all nations that are or would be free. We respect, no less, their independence. And when, in time of want or peril, they ask our help, they may honorably receive it; for we no more seek to buy their sovereignty than we would sell our own. Sovereignty is never bartered among freemen . . ."

[1] *Dwight D. Eisenhower became the tenth General to win the presidency. The others were Garfield, Hayes, Grant, W. H. Harrison, Taylor, Jackson, and Washington, Pierce & Benjamin Harrison. Four other generals were defeated in their bids for the office: Winfield Scott, John C. Fremont, Winfield S. Hancock, and George B. McClellan.*

1960

Losing Candidate: RICHARD M. NIXON[1]

(1913-) of California

Running Mate: Henry Cabot Lodge
Party: Republican
Convention: Chicago
Popular Vote: 34,108,546
Electoral Vote: 219

NIXON IS THE MAN FOR ME

Words and Music by
J. Maloy Roach
(ASCAP)

©Copyright, 1960, by J. Maloy Roach

PREVIOUS OCCUPATIONS

Navy
Lawyer
Politician
Congressman (1946-1950)
Senator (1950-1952)
Vice President (1952-1960)

---

[1] *Nixon became the first candidate to campaign in all fifty states.*

President: *JOHN F. KENNEDY*

1960

(1917-1963) of Massachusetts

"THE NEW FRONTIER"

Vice-President:
Lyndon B. Johnson[1]
Party: Democrat

Convention: Los Angeles
Popular Vote: 34,227,096
Electoral Vote: 303

PREVIOUS OCCUPATIONS

Navy
Congressman
Senator

EXCERPT FROM INAUGURAL ADDRESS, JANUARY 20, 1961:

". . . So let us begin anew — remembering on both sides that civility is not a sign of weakness, and sincerity is always subject to proof. *Let us never negotiate out of fear. But let us never fear to negotiate.*

"Let both sides explore what problems unite us instead of laboring those problems which divide us.

"Let both sides, for the first time, formulate serious and precise proposals for the inspection and control of arms—and bring the absolute power to destroy other nations under the absolute control of all nations.

"Let both sides seek to invoke the wonders of science instead of its terrors. Together let us explore the stars, conquer the deserts, eradicate disease, tap the ocean depths, and encourage the arts and commerce.

"Let both sides unite to heed in all corners of the earth the command of Isaiah—to 'undo the heavy burdens and to let the oppressed go free.' . . ."

---

[1]*Lyndon Baines Johnson becomes 36th President after the assassination of John F. Kennedy on November 22, 1963.*

1964

Losing Candidate: BARRY M. GOLDWATER

(1909-   ) of Arizona

OCCUPATION OF CANDIDATE:
Businessman (Department Store)

POLITICAL OFFICE HELD:
U. S. Senator from Arizona

Running Mate:
William Miller
Party: Republican
Convention: San Francisco
Popular Vote: 27,176,799
Electoral Vote: 52

GO WITH GOLDWATER

Words by
Tom McDonnell

Otis Clements
(ASCAP)

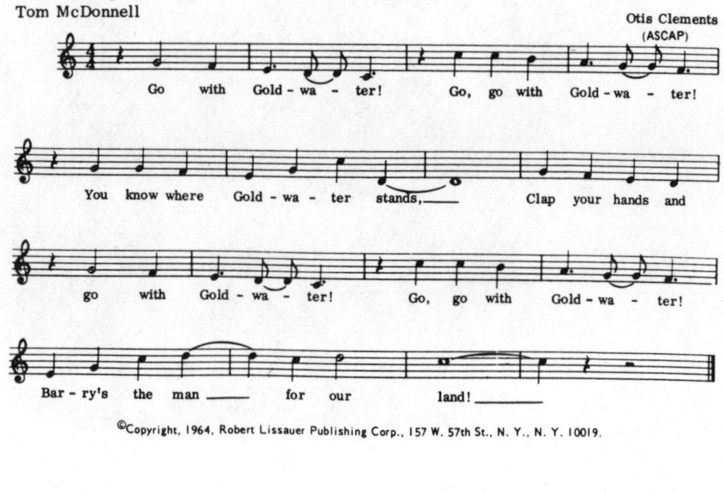

©Copyright, 1964, Robert Lissauer Publishing Corp., 157 W. 57th St., N. Y., N. Y. 10019.

President:
LYNDON B. JOHNSON[1]
(1908-1973) of Texas

1964

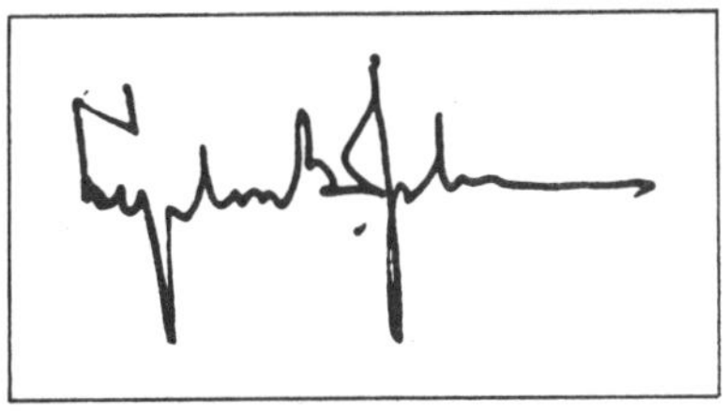

PREVIOUS OCCUPATIONS
Navy
Congressman
Senator
Vice President

"THE GREAT SOCIETY"

EXCERPT FROM INAUGURAL ADDRESS, JANUARY 20, 1965:

". . . How incredible it is that in this fragile existence we should hate and destroy one another. There are possibilities enough for all who will abandon mastery over others to pursue mastery over nature. There is world enough for all to seek their happiness in their own way . . . We aspire to nothing that belongs to others. We seek no dominion over our fellow man, but man's dominion over tyranny and misery . . ."

Vice-President:
Hubert H. Humphrey
Party: Democrat
Convention: Atlantic City
Popular Vote: 43,126,506
Electoral Vote: 486

[1]*Lyndon Johnson was the fourteenth President who had served in the U.S. Senate earlier in his career.*

1968

HUMPHREY
MUSKIE

Losing Candidate:
HUBERT HUMPHREY
(1911-1978) of South Dakota

OCCUPATIONS OF CANDIDATE
Pharmacist
College Teacher
Mayor (Minneapolis)
Senator (1948-1960)
Vice-President
Senator (1970-1979)

Running Mate: Edmund S. Muskie
Party: Democrat [1]

Convention: Chicago
Popular Vote: 31,275,165
Electoral Vote: 191

---

[1] *A strong Third-Party bid was made in this election by the American Independent Party led by George Wallace of Alabama and his running mate, Curtis LeMay. The AIP won 9,906,473 popular votes and 46 electoral votes.*

1968

President: RICHARD M. NIXON [1]

(1913-) of California

Vice-President: Spiro T. Agnew
Party: Republican
Convention: Miami Beach
Popular Vote: 31,785,480
Electoral Vote: 301

EXCERPT FROM 1st INAUGURAL ADDRESS, JAN. 20, 1969

We seek an open world — open to ideas, open to the exchange of goods and people, a world in which no people, great or small, will live in angry isolation.

We cannot expect to make everyone our friend, but we can try to make no one our enemy.

Those who would be our adversaries, we invite to a peaceful competition — not in conquering territory or extending dominion, but in enriching the life of man.

As we explore the reaches of space, let us go to the new worlds together — not as new worlds to be conquered, but as a new adventure to be shared.

[1] *Nixon was the third man to have been defeated in his first attempt at the presidency, and then subsequently elected in a second attempt. The others were Andrew Jackson and William Henry Harrison.*

1972

Losing Candidate: *GEORGE McGOVERN*

(1922-   ) of South Dakota

OCCUPATIONS OF CANDIDATE
College Professor
Congressman
Senator

Running Mate: Sargent Shriver
Party: Democrat

Convention: Miami Beach
Popular Vote: 29,170,774
Electoral Vote: 17

1972

President: RICHARD M. NIXON

Vice-President: Spiro T. Agnew[1]

Party: Republican

Convention: Miami Beach

Popular Vote: 47,165,234

Electoral Vote: 520

EXCERPT FROM SECOND INAUGURAL ADDRESS, JAN. 20, 1973[2]

"... Let us build a structure of peace in the world in which the weak are as safe as the strong, in which each respects the right of the other to live by a different system, in which those who would influence others will do so by the strength of their ideas and not by the force of their arms.

... Government must learn to take less from the people so that people can do more for themselves. Let us remember that America was built not by government but by people, not by welfare, but by work, not by shirking responsibility, but by seeking responsibility.

... America's record in this century has been unparalleled in the world's history for its responsibility, for its generosity, for its creativity, and for its progress.

Let us be proud that our system has produced and provided more freedom and more abundance, more widely shared, than any system in the history of the world.

[1]*Spiro T. Agnew resigns as Vice-President on Oct. 10, 1973, and President Nixon appoints Gerald R. Ford, Republican Congressman from Michigan, to the vacant position.*

[2]*Richard M. Nixon resigns the presidency on August 8, 1974; he is succeeded by Gerald R. Ford who becomes the first man in the history of the United States to reach both the offices of the Vice-President and the President without having been elected. President Ford then fills the vacant post of the Vice-President by appointing Nelson R. Rockefeller.*

1976

Losing Candidate: Gerald R. Ford[1]

(1913-) of Nebraska

Running Mate: Robert J. Dole

Party: Republican

Convention: Kansas City

Popular Vote: 39,148,940

Electoral Vote: 240

EXCERPT FROM STATE OF THE UNION ADDRESS, JAN. 15, 1975

"...Let us mobilize the most powerful and most creative industrial nation that ever existed on this earth to put all our people to work. The emphasis on our economic efforts must now shift from inflation to jobs.

...As we move forward to meet our global challenges and opportunities, we must have the tools to do the job... Military strength alone is not sufficient. Effective diplomacy is also essential in preventing conflict, in building world understanding.

...As our 200th anniversary approaches, we owe it to ourselves and to posterity to rebuild our political and economic strength. Let us make America again and for centuries more to come what it has so long been — a stronghold and a beacon-light of liberty for the whole world.

PREVIOUS OCCUPATIONS

Navy
Politician (Congressman 25 yrs)
Only man to be appointed to both Vice Presidency & Presidency

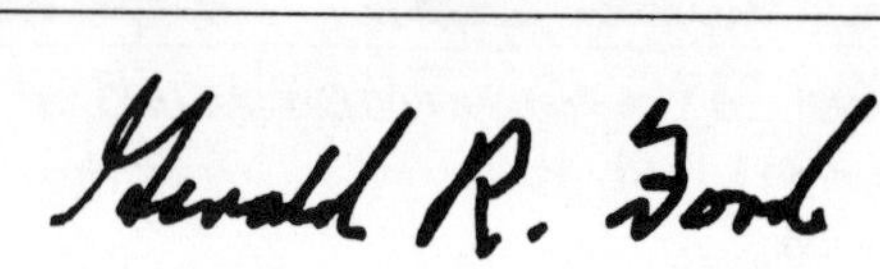

[1] *When Gerald Ford became President, he was the 27th man to hold the office who had graduated from Law School, or had read Law as a profession.*

1976

President: *JIMMY CARTER*

(1924-   ) of Georgia

Vice-President:
Walter Mondale
Party: Democrat
Convention:
New York City
Popular Vote:
40,826,629
Electoral Vote: 297

EXCERPT FROM INAUGURAL ADDRESS, JAN. 20, 1977

The passion for freedom is on the rise. Tapping this new spirit, there can be no nobler nor more ambitious task for America to undertake on this day of a new beginning than to help shape a just and peaceful world that is truly humane. We are a strong nation and we will maintain strength so sufficient that it need not be proven in combat — a quiet strength based not merely on the size of an arsenal, but on the nobility of ideas. We will be ever vigilant and never vulnerable, and we will fight our wars against poverty, ignorance and injustice, for those are the enemies against which our forces can be honorably marshalled. We are a proudly idealistic nation, but let no one confuse our idealism with weakness. Because we are free we can never be indifferent to the fate of freedom elsewhere. Our moral sense dictates a clearcut preference for those societies which share with us an abiding respect for individual human rights. We do not seek to intimidate, but it is clear that a world which others can dominate with impunity would be inhospitable to decency and a threat to the well-being of all people.

PREVIOUS OCCUPATIONS

Navy (Career Officer)
Farmer
Politician (Governor)

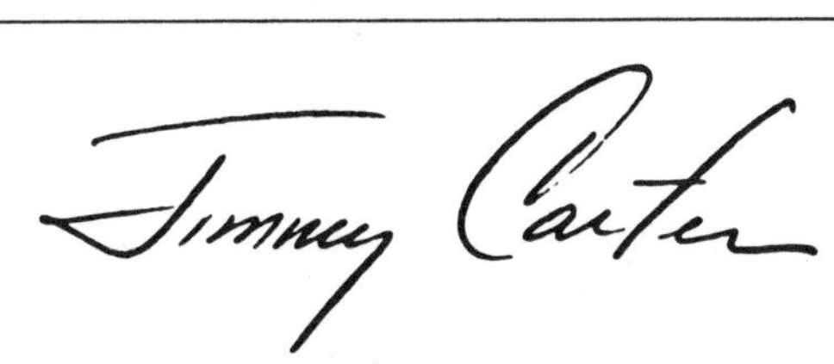

1980

Losing Candidate: *JIMMY CARTER*[1]

Running Mate:
Walter Mondale
Party: Democrat[2]
Convention: New York City
Popular Vote: 35,481,435
Electoral Vote: 49

DEMOCRATIC PARTY

---

[1] *Jimmy Carter was the ninth president who was defeated in his bid for re-election. The others were John Adams, John Quincy Adams, Martin van Buren, Grover Cleveland, Benjamin Harrison, Teddy Roosevelt, Herbert Hoover, and Gerald Ford.*

[2] *John Anderson won 5,719,437 popular votes in a third party bid for the presidency. He was the candidate of the Independent Party.*

1980

President: *Ronald Reagan*[1]

(1911-) of Illinois

Vice-President: George Bush
Party: Republican
Convention: Detroit
Popular Vote: 43,899,248
Electoral Vote: 489

PREVIOUS OCCUPATIONS

Actor
Governor - State Legislature[2]

EXCERPT FROM INAUGURAL ADDRESS, JAN. 20, 1981

It is my intention to curb the size and influence of the Federal establishment and to demand recognition of the distinction between the powers granted to the Federal Government and those reserved to the States or to the people. All of us need to be reminded that the Federal Government did not create the States; the States created the Federal Government. If we look to the answer as to why for so many years we achieved so much, prospered as no other people on Earth, it was because here in this land we unleashed the energy and individual genius of man to a greater extent than has ever been done before. Freedom and the dignity of the individual have been more available and assured here than in any other place on Earth. The price for this freedom at times has been high. But we have never been unwilling to pay that price. As for the enemies of freedom, those who are potential adversaries, they will be reminded that peace is the highest aspiration of the American people. We will negotiate for it, sacrifice for it; we will not surrender for it now or ever.

[1] *At the age of sixty-nine, Ronald Reagan was the oldest man to achieve the Presidency. Seven other men were sixty or older when elected: William Henry Harrison, 68; James Buchanan, 65; Zachary Taylor, 64; John Adams, Gerald R. Ford, and Andrew Jackson were all 61; and Dwight D. Eisenhower was 60.*

[2] *Ronald Reagan was the eighteenth man elected to the Presidency who had at one time served in the office of State Governor.*

Wyoming — Caucus, March, date uncertain
Virgin Islands — Caucus, date uncertain
Guam — Caucus, date uncertain

May 24 — Idaho (C)
June 5 — California (P)
New Jersey (P)
New Mexico (P)
New Dakota (P)
Ohio (P)
South Dakota (P)
West Virginia (P)
June 9 — Virgin Island (C)
Dates Not Set — Nevada (C)
Wyoming (C)
Democrats Abroad
Guam
Latin America

*=Date Not Settled

CONVENTION RESULTS

DEMOCRATIC CONVENTION - JULY 16-20
SAN FRANCISCO, CALIFORNIA

BALLOT

CANDIDATE	1	2	3	4	5	6	7	8

REPUBLICAN CONVENTION - AUGUST 20-30
DALLAS, TEXAS

BALLOT

CANDIDATE	1	2	3	4	5	6	7	8

NOVEMBER 6 ELECTION RESULTS

________ (For President) and ________ (For Vice-President) vs. ________ (For President) and ________ (For Vice-President)

Popular vote ________ **Popular vote** ________

Electoral vote ________ **Electoral vote** ________

President-Elect ________ **Vice-President-Elect** ________

STATE PRIMARY AND CAUCUS RESULTS

DEMOCRATIC PRIMARIES

DATE	STATE	WINNING CANDIDATE
February 27	Iowa (C)*	
March 6	New Hampshire (P)*	
March 13	Massachusetts (P)	
	Alabama (P)	
	Florida (P)	
	Georgia (P)	
	Oklahoma (C)	
	Washington (C)	
	Rhode Island (P)	
	Democrats Abroad (MIP)	
	Hawaii (C)	
March 14	Delaware (C)	
	Alaska (C)	
March 17	Mississippi (C)	
	Latin America (C)	
	South Carolina (C)	
	Arkansas (C)	
	Michigan (C)	
	Kentucky (C)	
	North Dakota (14-28)	
March 18	Peurto Rico (P)	
March 19	Virginia (C)	
March 20	Illinois (P)	
	Minnesota (C)	
March 24	Kansas (C)	
March 25	Montana (C)	
March 27	Connecticut (P)	
March 31	Wisconsin (if primary 4/3)	
April 7	Louisiana (P)	
April 4	Arizona (C)	
April 16	Utah (C)	
April 17	Missouri (C)	
April 24	Vermont (C)	
	Pennsylvania (P)	
May 1	District of Columbia (P)	
	Tennessee (P)	
May 5	Texas (C)	
May 7	Colorado (C)	
May 8	Indiana (P)	
	North Carolina (P)	
	Maryland (P)	
	Ohio (P)	
May 15	Nebraska (P)	
	Oregon (P)	
May 22	New York (P)	
May 24	Idaho (C)	
June 5	California (P)	
	New Jersey (P)	
	New Mexico (P)	
	South Dakota (P)	
	West Virginia (P)	
Others:		
Maine	— Caucus, requesting exemption for March 4, CRC to evaluate.	
Nevada	— Caucus, date uncertain	

REPUBLICAN PRIMARIES

DATE	STATE	WINNING CANDIDATE
February 13	Iowa (C)*	
February 20	Iowa (C)	
February 27	Iowa (C)	
February 28	New Hampshire (P)**	
March 4	Maine Caucus	
March 6	Vermont (P) (Beauty Contest)	
	New Hampshire (P)	
March 13	Alabama (P)	
	Florida (P)	
	Georgia (P)	
	Massachusetts (P)	
	Rhode Island (P)	
	Tennessee (P)	
	Hawaii (C)	
	Oaklahoma (C)	
	Washington (C)	
	Alaska (C)	
March 14	Delaware (C)	
March 17	Arkansas (C)	
	Latin America (C)	
	Kentucky (C)	
	Michigan (C)	
	Mississippi (C)	
	South Carolina (C)	
	Tennessee (C)	
March 18	Puerto Rico (P)	
March 19	Virginia (C)	
March 20	Illinois (P)	
	Minnesota (C)	
March 24	Kansas (C)	
	Virginia (C)	
March 25	Montana (C)	
March 27	Connecticut (P)	
March 31	Wisconsin (C)	
April 3	Wisconsin (P)	
April 7	Louisiana (P)	
April 14	Arizona (C)	
April 16	Utah (C)	
April 17	Alaska (P)	
	Missouri (C)	
April 24	Pennsylvania (P)	
	Vermont (C)	
May 1	D. C. (P)	
May 5	Texas (P)	
	Texas (C)	
May 7	Colorado (C)	
May 8	Indiana (P)	
	Maryland (P)	
	North Carolina (P)	
	Tennessee (P)	
May 15	Nebraska (P)	
	Oregon (P)	
May 22	Idaho (P)	
	New York (P)	

...and "Third Parties"

One of the most interesting events of each presidential campaign is the emergence of one or more of the "Third Parties." Some, like the Anti-Monopoly, are short lived; others, like the Socialist (whose perennial leader Norman Thomas is pictured above), are firmly entrenched in American politics. A Third Party may have vague ideals like the Continental; it may be a magnet for discontented members of a larger party (e.g., the Christian Nationalist of 1948); or it may be a coalition of intellectuals and reformers demanding that the federal government take a more direct hand in bettering the human condition like the Socialists or Socialist-Laborites.

Furthermore, some Third Parties are nothing more than factions of the major parties and are never heard of after the election. Several of these factions have unforgettable names like Mugwumps, Barnburners, or Locofocos. Sometimes a faction develops into a Third Party, as when members of the 1948 Dixiecrat faction of the Democrats formed the States' Rights Party because its extreme conservatism could not find a voice in the major parties.

In any case, Third Parties are given a separate section in this book because, unlike banners, buttons, slogans, and songs, they are not always mere campaign ephemera – they are sometimes concrete manifestations of opposition to the major parties.

THIRD PARTIES AND FACTIONS OF U.S. POLITICAL HISTORY

...A SHORT LEXICON

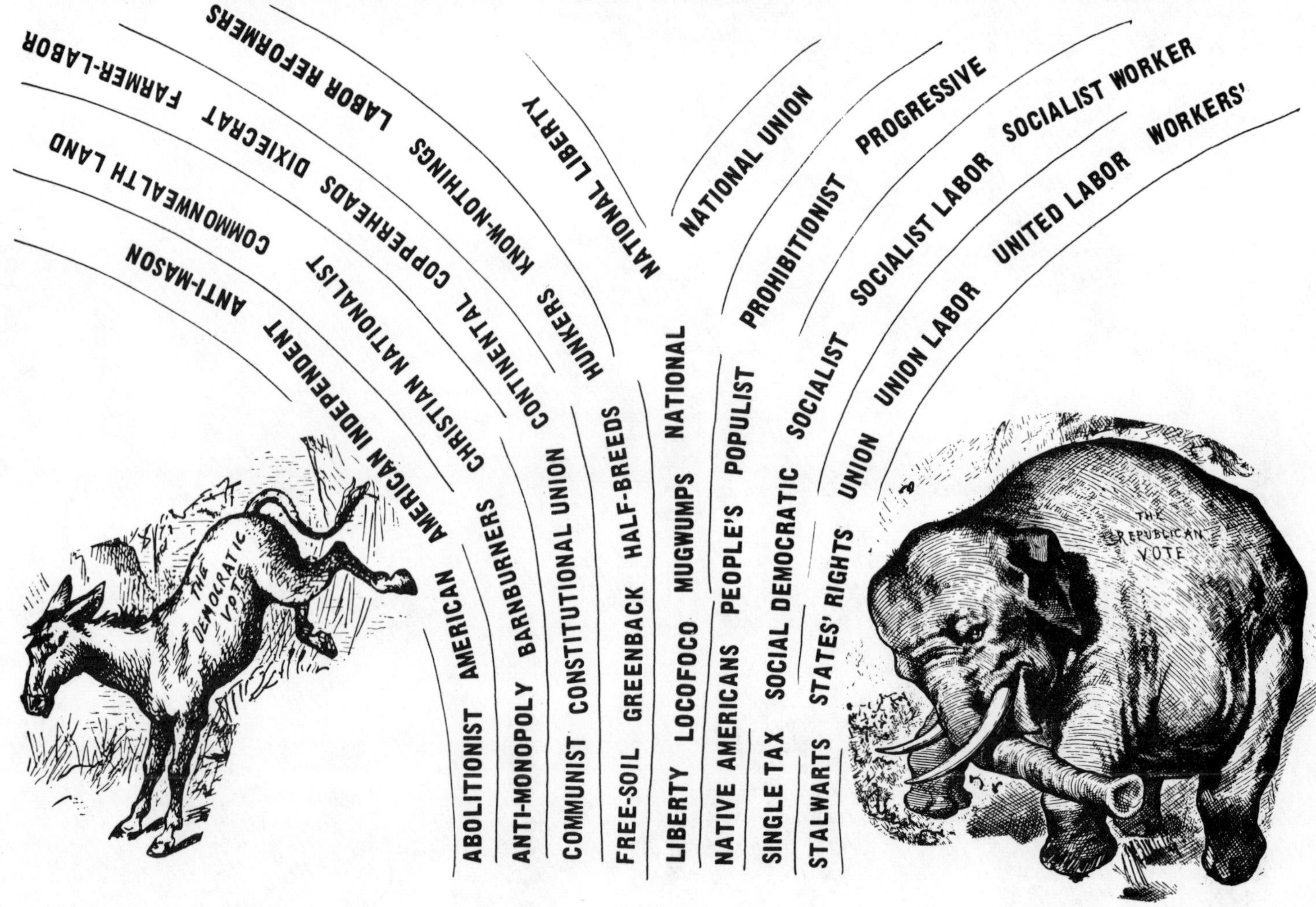

ABOLITIONIST: This party (properly called Liberty Party) was against slavery. The Liberty Party held conventions and nominated James G. Birney for the presidency in the elections of 1840 and 1844.

AMERICAN: This party was organized in 1924 and held a convention in Columbus. Gilbert O. Nations was nominated for the presidency. The party advocated that a Federal Office of Education be established in the President's Cabinet.

AMERICAN INDEPENDENT: This party is led by George Wallace of Alabama. See Dixiecrat and Christian Nationalist.

ANTI-MASON: This party was against secret societies such as the Masons. Also of primary concern was their opposition to Jackson. They convened in Baltimore in 1831 and nominated William Wirt for the presidency.

ANTI-MONOPOLY: Paragraph two of the Anti-Monopoly Party's platform aptly sums up their main plank: "That corporations, the creatures of law, should be controlled by law." The convention was held in Chicago in 1884 and Benjamin F. Butler was nominated for the presidency.

BARNBURNERS: This was a faction of the Democratic Party interested in reforms during Polk's administration. They said they were so bent on achieving reforms that they were willing to imitate the Dutch farmer who would burn his barn to exterminate the rats that infested it.

CHRISTIAN NATIONALIST: In 1948 and 1952 this party put forth a platform advocating a return to the "Cross and the Flag" and denounced the country's socialistic tendencies.

COMMONWEALTH LAND: Convening in New York in 1924, the Commonwealth Land Party nominated William J. Wallace for the presidency. Their poetically phrased platform culminates to a resounding climax in the last paragraph: "If civilization is to live, private ownership of land must go. If private ownership of land continues, this civilization is doomed."

COMMUNIST: The last platform of the Communist Party was printed in 1948; the last national election they entered was in 1940. For further information see Workers' Party.

CONSTITUTIONAL UNION: The Constitutional Union Party was organized to hold the Union together. Their platform was interesting because of its condemnation of "platforms" and its simple statement to uphold the Constitution. They convened in Baltimore in 1860 and nominated John Bell for the presidency.

CONTINENTAL: In 1904 this party convened in Chicago to "unite the disaffected of all parties," and nominated Austin H. Holcomb for the office of President. In their platform they "demand the enactment . . . of a primary election law, by which all candidates for public office shall be selected by direct vote of the people without the aid of a delegate convention."

COPPERHEADS: During the Civil War the Northern Democrats were split into two factions: the "War" faction or those who abided by the principles of Stephen A. Douglas to continue the war to preserve the Union; and the "Peace" faction whose principles dictated peace first, union second. In the ranks of the "Peace" Democrats there was a group of Confederate sympathizers, who because of their moral and material support to the Confederacy, were called Copperheads. Copperheads who were caught giving material support were prosecuted for treason.

DIXIECRAT: This States' Rights faction of the Democratic Party was made up of dissenting Southern voters. In 1948 they gave 1,169,021 votes to Strom Thurmond. In 1960 Orville Faubus received a scattered number of votes for the presidency. The new leader of those who favor a stronger States' Rights position is former Governor George Wallace of Alabama.

FARMER-LABOR: The Farmer-Labor Party first participated in national politics in 1920 and put forth candidates and platforms in each election up to and including 1932. In their 1932 platform they advocated free coinage of silver and demanded that "Germany should print 11½ billions of full legal tender currency" and pay off its war debts to foreign nations "that are likewise indebted to the United States."

FREE-SOIL: The Free-Soil Party was instituted to oppose the extension of slavery into new areas. They feared that slave labor would undermine free labor. In their platform of 1848 they coined the famous slogan which permeated the entire election: "Free Soil, Free Speech, Free Labor, and Free Men." Their nominee for the presidency was Martin Van Buren. They took enough votes away from the Democrats to enable the Whigs to elect Zachary Taylor.

GREENBACK: The Greenbacks advocated printing paper money ("greenbacks") as needed, with little concern as to whether the money was properly backed by gold or silver. In 1876 they nominated Peter Cooper, in 1880 James B. Weaver, and in 1884 Benjamin F. Butler for the presidential office.

HALF-BREEDS: This was the Reform half of the 1880 Republican Party and was led by James G. Blaine. They backed James A. Garfield for President and compromised with the "Stalwarts" by agreeing to run Chester A. Arthur as the Vice-President on the party ticket.

HUNKERS: During Polk's administration a faction of the Democratic Party was so called because they "hunkered" after office.

KNOW-NOTHINGS: "Know-Nothings" were also known as "Native Americans." They advocated that "Americans must rule America," meaning that they were against foreign-born

Americans. They were also decidedly anti-Catholic. They received their nickname because when asked anything about their organization they professed to "know nothing." In 1856 they nominated former President Millard Fillmore. They disappeared after 1856.

LABOR REFORMERS: The Labor Reformers nominated Charles O'Conor in 1872 for the office of President. The party was made up of tradesmen and was developed from "The Knights of St. Crispin," a shoemakers' union. The members protested the use of Chinese labor and were in favor of the eight-hour working day for all "mechanics and laborers" hired by the government, whether federal, state, or municipal.

LIBERTY: The official name of the Abolitionist Party. See Abolitionist.

LOCOFOCO: The Equal Rights faction of the Democratic Party was so christened by the opposition in 1835 after an incident in Tammany Hall. All the lights were purposely extinguished by the departing Tammany men and the Equal Righters continued the meeting by lighting candles with the newly invented matches called locofocos.

MUGWUMPS: In 1884 the Republicans who threw their support to the Democratic candidate Grover Cleveland were said to be sitting on the "political fence" with their "mugs" on one side and their "wumps" on the other. Their defection helped to elect Cleveland.

NATIONAL: In 1896 this group split from the Prohibitionists and nominated Charles E. Bentley for the presidency. In their platform they advocated that the President, Vice-President, and U. S. Senate be elected by direct vote; that railroads and telegraph systems be operated by the government; that women be allowed to vote; that silver be coined at a ratio of 16 to 1; and that alcoholic beverages be abolished.

NATIONAL LIBERTY: This party was formed by a group of Negroes and held a convention in St. Louis in 1904; they nominated George E. Taylor for the presidency. In their platform they pathetically note with regret that the two great parties could "overlook lynching, and yet denounce polygamy." The platform also makes an impassioned plea to the Catholic and Protestant religions "to assist us to awaken the Christian consciences of all classes of American people . . ."

NATIONAL UNION: This was the name given to the Republican Party during the 1864 election because of the merger of Union League members with Republicans. The name as well as the merger was effected by the wording of the invitation to the Republican Convention to all persons, regardless of former party affiliations, who would stand by the present administration and who "desire the unconditional maintenance of the Union . . ."

NATIVE AMERICANS: Another name for the Know-Nothings.

PEOPLE'S: Another name for the Populist Party.

POPULIST: The Populist Party was organized in 1891 and consisted mainly of farmers from the South and the West. They advocated currency inflation and free coinage of silver. In 1892 they nominated James B. Weaver for the presidency, and in 1896 they backed William Jennings Bryan. They gradually disbanded after Bryan's first defeat.

PROHIBITIONIST: The Prohibitionists advocated the abolishment of alcoholic beverages. They have nominated a candidate in every election since 1872 and to this day have a National Committee. In 1967 at their national convention in Detroit they nominated E. Harold Munn as their candidate for the 1968 presidential campaign.

PROGRESSIVE: The name "Progressives" has sheltered within its confines such widely diversified individuals as Theodore Roosevelt, Robert La Follette, and recently (1948) Henry Wallace. In each instance "Progressive" was a different party.

In 1912 Teddy Roosevelt bolted from the Republican Party of Taft and formed his Progressive Party (The Bull-Moosers). This faction became the most powerful Third Party in American history, gathering more popular votes than the Republican Party and enabling the Democrats to elect Wilson. This Progressive Party dissipated after the election.

The "second" Progressive Party was formed under the aegis of Senator Robert La Follette of Wisconsin and in 1924 was made up of the more socialistic members of the Republican Party, along with two other progressive groups (Socialist and Farmer-Labor). Although they did well in the popular vote (4,826,471), they were far outdistanced by both the Republicans and the Democrats. After their failure to achieve the presidency, this group of Progressives also disbanded and rejoined the major parties.

The "third" Progressive Party was formed in 1948 by Democratic dissidents and Communist sympathizers who held a convention in Philadelphia and nominated former Vice-President Henry Wallace as their presidential candidate. The "third" Progressives emerged a very poor fourth in the balloting with a mere 1,157,172 popular vote and no electoral votes.

SINGLE TAX: Another name for the Commonwealth Land Party used during the 1920 campaign.

SOCIAL DEMOCRATIC: The name used by the Socialist Party in 1900.

SOCIALIST: In 1900 the Socialists (then known as Social Democrats) nominated Eugene V. Debs for the presidency. Debs was subsequently nominated in every election up to and including 1920 (with the exception of 1916). In 1924 the Socialists backed Robert La Follette and the Progressives. From 1928 to 1948 Norman Thomas received the nomination. No candidate was put forth in 1960 or 1964. The Socialist Party was advocating Social Security measures thirty years before the "New Deal" and have long advocated bills for better housing and better education subsidized by federal money. They have long campaigned for civil rights, fair wages, and fair working conditions, and have at times been an effective conscience to the two major parties.

SOCIALIST LABOR: The Socialist Labor Party has held conventions and run candidates since 1892. They are distinct from the Socialist Party of Debs and Thomas. Although they might be called radical socialists, their platforms, along with the Socialists, are sometimes provocative documents of humane thought. For example, the 1916 platform reads: ". . . migratory farm workers badly need the help of organized labor to build the unions they have started . . ."; in a later section, ". . . enact and enforce legislation to abolish lynching, the poll tax, and all forms of segregation . . ." and "combat all forms of anti-Semitism."

SOCIALIST WORKER: This vigorously anti-war, pro-racial equality, and anti-capitalist party nominated for the 1968 campaign Fred Halstead for President and Paul Boutelle for Vice-President, both of New York.

STALWARTS: This was a conservative section of the 1880 Republicans led by Senator Roscoe Conkling. They backed Chester A. Arthur and were appeased by his nomination for the vice-presidency.

STATES' RIGHTS: See American Independent, Christian Nationalist, and Dixiecrat.

UNION: This short-lived party gathered over 900,000 votes in 1936. Among other things their platform advocated Congressional legislation to assure a living annual wage ". . . for all laborers capable of working and willing to work." The party was a coalition of anti-Roosevelt forces led by Dr. Francis Townsend, Father Coughlin, and Gerald Smith. Their candidate was William Lemke.

UNION LABOR: This was one of the two factions of the 1888 Labor Party (Labor Reformers). They held a convention in Cincinnati and nominated Alson J. Streeter for the presidency. In their platform they advocated graduated income tax, direct election of senators, and the enactment of legislation to exclude Chinese from the U. S.

UNITED LABOR: This was the other faction of the 1888 Labor Party (see Union Labor above). They met in Cincinnati and nominated Robert H. Cowdrey for the presidency. Their platform stated, among other things, that they wished to ". . . give all men an interest in the land of their country; to enable all to share in the benefits of social growth and improvement . . . to do away with the monstrous injustice which deprives producers of the fruits of their toil while idlers grow rich . . ."

WORKERS': The American Communist Party, upon entering the national political elections, was identified as the Workers' Party. In 1924 they convened in Cleveland and nominated William Zebulon Foster for the presidency. In the 1924 platform they denounced Coolidge as a "strike-breaker," Davis as a "Morgan-Rockefeller lawyer," and La Follette as a supporter of the "Capitalist system of exploitation." In the same document they advocated revolution which would "create a Soviet government and the dictatorship of the proletariat." In 1932 they adopted the name "Communist."

ACKNOWLEDGMENTS

The author wishes to thank the following individuals, institutions, and publishers for their kind permission to use the photographs, illustrations, cartoons, and songs listed below.

IRVING BERLIN MUSIC CORPORATION: "I Like Ike" (song), 1952.
BOWDOIN COLLEGE LIBRARY: "Have You Heard from Maine" (song), 1896.
BROWN UNIVERSITY, HARRIS COLLECTION: "Cass and Butler" (text only), 1848; "Gallant Scott Is Our Choice" (text only), 1852 "Democratic Battle Hymn" (text only), 1852; "Good-bye Teddy. You Must March." (song), 1904.
LIBRARY OF CONGRESS: George Washington (1789); John Adams (1796); Thomas Jefferson (1800); James Madison (1808); James Monroe (1816); John Quincy Adams (1824); Andrew Jackson (1828); Henry Clay (1832); "King Andrew the First" (cartoon) (1832); "Grand Match Between the Kinderhook Poney and the Ohio Ploughman" (1836); William Henry Harrison (1836) William Henry Harrison (1840); Martin Van Buren (1840); James K. Polk (1844); Zachary Taylor (1848); Winfield Scott (1852); Franklin Pierce (1852); James Buchanan (1856); "Vanity Fair" cartoon (1860); Stephen A. Douglas (1860); Lewis Cass (1848); Abraham Lincoln (1864); George B. McLellan (1864); Horatio Seymour (1868); Horace Greeley (1872); Rutherford B. Hayes (1876); Samuel Tilden (1876); Thomas Hendricks (1876); James A. Garfield (1880); Winfield S. Hancock (1880); James G. Blaine (1884); Inauguration of President Cleveland (1884); Grover Cleveland (1888); Benjamin Harrison (1888); "The Raven" (1892); William McKinley (1900); Chief Justice Fuller Administering the Oath of Office (1896); Alton B. Parker (1904); Woodrow Wilson (1912-1916); Herbert Hoover (1928); Wendell Willkie (1940); Gerald R. Ford (1976); Jimmy Carter (1976); Ronald Reagan (1980).
ROBERT LISSAUER PUBLISHING CORPORATION: "Believe in Stevenson" (song), 1956; "Go With Goldwater" (song), 1964.
ROACH, J. MALOY: "Nixon Is The Man For Me" (song), 1960.
RYSKIND, MORRIE: "We Like Willkie" (song lyrics), 1940.
SHAPIRO, BERNSTEIN & COMPANY, INC.: "Wilson, That's All" (song), 1916.
SMITHSONIAN INSTITUTION: Invitation to Jackson's Inaugural Ball, (1828); John C. Fremont (1856); Detail of an 1856 Democratic Ballot; Harrison Medal (1888); Wm. Jennings Bryan Ribbon (1900); Warren G. Harding Button (1920); "Keep Cool-idge" Poster (1924); Al Smith Ribbon (1928); FDR Ribbon (1940); Adlai Stevenson Button (1956); Gerald R. Ford Button (1976); Jimmy Carter Buttons (1980).
UNITED PRESS INTERNATIONAL: Theodore Roosevelt (1904); Wm. Jennings Bryan (1908); Wm. Howard Taft (1908-1912); Charles Evans Hughes (1916); James M. Cox (1920); Cox and Roosevelt Ribbon (1920); Calvin Coolidge (1924); John W. Davis (1924); Al Smith (1928); Herbert Hoover (1932); F.D.R. and John Nance Garner (1936); Alf Landon (1936); F.D.R. (1944); Republican Convention (Dewey Signs) (1944); Convention Ribbon (1944); Thomas E. Dewey (1948); Harry S. Truman (1948); Dwight D. Eisenhower (1952); Republican Convention (1956); Adlai E. Stevenson (1952); John F. Kennedy (1960); Richard M. Nixon (1960); Lyndon B. Johnson (1964); Barry Goldwater (1964); Richard M. Nixon (1968); Richard M. Nixon (1972); George McGovern (1972); Norman Thomas and . . . Third Parties.
CARNEGIE LIBRARY: John Tyler (1840); Millard Fillmore (1848); Abraham Lincoln (1860); Andrew Johnson (1864); Ulysses S. Grant (1868-1872); Chester A. Arthur (1880); F.D.R. (1940).
OTHER: William Jennings Bryan (1896) — Cincinnati Enquirer; Theodore Roosevelt (1912) — Sagamore Hill National Historic Site, Oyster Bay, New York; Franklin Delano Roosevelt (1932 & 1940) — Associated Press; Jimmy Carter (1980); Hubert H. Humphrey (1968) — Valley Daily News; Humphrey-Muskie button from Private Collections; Nixon button from Private Collections; McGovern button from Private Collections; Reagan buttons from Private Collections.

A special thanks is due to the following persons and institutions for their assistance in the location of various materials used in BANNERS, BUTTONS AND SONGS; David Williams and the photo department of the Valley Daily News, Tarentum, Pa.; Joe Luppino of United Press International; the staff of the Library of Congress; the staff of the Smithsonian Institution; the staff of the Main Branch of the Toronto Public Library, Toronto, Canada; Helen Reilly; Michael Rutherford of Welch & Quest Limited; Peggy Dusch of Carnegie Library; and a very special thanks to the person who urged and encouraged me to revise, update, and republish this book, and who went on all the photo-seeking forays with no complaints — my wife Roberta.